CHRONICLES OF OLD NEW YORK

EXPLORING MANHATTAN'S LANDMARK NEIGHBORHOODS

Published in the United States by:
Museyon, Inc.
20 E. 46th St., Ste. 1400
New York, NY 10017

Museyon is a registered trademark.
Visit us online at www.museyon.com

Portions of this book were originally published in *New York Living* magazine.

ISBN 978-0-9822320-6-4

195910

Printed in China

It is said that New York City's life blood runs green, the color of money. But for those of us who carry on lifelong love affairs with this hyperactive island, the story is much more nuanced and colorful. When you read these chronicles you too will find in them a universal pride in human accomplishment—often in the face of adversity. Look for the genius, creativity, derring-do in every area of human endeavor, from economics to architecture, that have made and continue to imagine, one of the most fascinating human settlements on earth. And put this book on your favorite shelf, to be grabbed and read each time you decide to discover or rediscover one of our many and unique neighborhoods which, together, create the great metropolis.

—Susan S. Szenasy
Editor in Chief
Metropolis Magazine

View of New York from Brooklyn Heights, 1849

PLAN
DE NEW-YORK
et des Environs
Levé par Montresor Ingénieur en 1775.
A PARIS
Chez le Rouge rue des Grands Augustins
1777

PARTIE

DE

LONG ISLAND

West Bank   East Bank

Ranson River

NEW

JERSEY

HUDSON RIVIERE

RIVIERE DE L'EST

NOUVELLE YORK

Novum Eboracum, Capitale d'une Province de même
Nom dans la Nouvelle Angleterre en Amerique ci-devant
Nouvelle Amsterdam. Latitude Septent.le 40 Deg. 42 min.
Longitude 57 Deg. Hudson Anglois la decouvrit en 1608 cher-
chant un passage pour la Chine les Hollandois y construisi-
rent le Fort de Maçonnerie en 1613. le Front du Nord Est
est couvert d'un Ravelin plus nuisible qu'utile est comman-
dé par une hauteur a 150 pieds les Batteries qui
enveloppent ce Fort et la Pointe de l'Isle sont enfilées
de tout côté. 92 Embrasures sont occupées par 71.

RENVOI

a. Fort George	*m.* Attelier	*y.* Quakers
b. Batteries	*n.* College	*n.* Presbyteriens
c. Hôpital militaire	*o.* Marché	*&.* Sinagogue
d. Secretariat	*p.* Eglise de la Trinité	*1.* Anabaptistes
e. Magazin à Poudre	*q.* Chapelle S.t George	*2.* Morave
f. Parapiax	*r.* S.t Paul	*3.* Nouv.le Eglise Lutherienne
g. Porte, Quais	*s.* Anc.ne Eglise Hollandoise	*4.* Ecolle de la Ville
h. Construction	*t.* Nouv.le Eglise Hollandoise	*5.* Batterie Rimée
i. Halle	*u.* Eglise Lutherienne	*6.* Pompe fournissant
k. la Bourse	*w.* Calvinistes	*l'Eau a la Ville*
l. Prison	*x.* Protestans Francois	

Map of New York, 1775

For Ben Heilman

who taught me many

chronicles of old New York

Cities aren't built from bricks and steel alone.
It takes dreamers and schemers, visionaries
and risk-takers. For four centuries these
adventurous spirits have been drawn to New
York City, each leaving a mark that can still
be seen today. The history of Manhattan is
written in its streets; here's where to find it.

WALKING TOURS

APPENDIX

CHRONICLES OF OLD NEW YORK TIMELINE

1626 Peter Minuit buys Manahattan island from the Lenape

1763 Queen's Head Tavern opens

1781 Charles Cornwallis surrenders to George Washington

1783 New York City is liberated from British control

John Jacob Astor arrives in New York from Germany

1785 Congress moves to New York City
NYC population reaches 25,000

1786 City's first registry created at Merchants' Coffee House

1789 Washington Inaugurated at Federal Hall

1807 Aldermen implement urban plan, propose grid of numbered streets

1811 Uptown "grid" adopted and city land leveled

1822 All streets below City Hall deemed an "infected district" with smallpox, cholera, and yellow fever; population flees to rural Greenwich Village

1825 Gas lines laid for street lamps

1828 Washington Military Parade Grounds established; gallows torn down

1830 Public stagecoaches service begins

1831 New York University established

1834 Davy Crockett and the *New York Sun* publish exposes on life in the Five Points slums

1837 New York University builds Gothic Revival campus on Washington Square

1840 First portrait photograph in sunlight taken at NYU

1841 Charles Dickens reports on life in Five Points

Grace Church built by James Renwick

1848 City's population reaches 515,000

John Jacob Astor dies

James Bogardus builds the city's first cast-iron building

1849 Riots at Astor Place Opera House

1852 Fifth Avenue "opened"— graded and paved

^View of New York, after 1883

1857	Otis brothers introduce elevators; the skyscraper is born
1858	Richard Morris Hunt designs Tenth Street Studio
1869	Lord & Taylor opens on Ladies' Mile
	Freight terminal opens on Lower West Side
1870	Jacob Riis arrives in New York from Denmark
1879	Saint Patrick's Cathedral is dedicated
1880	Thomas Edison demonstrates his incandescent light bulb
1882	Edison turns on the lights at 23 Wall Street
	Congress passes the Chinese Exclusion Act
1888	Five Points becomes most densely populated neighborhood in the world with 335,000 people per square mile; the infant mortality rate on Mulberry Street reaches 68 percent
1889	Centennial of Washington's inauguration celebrated with a temporary wooden arch in Washington Square
	Jacob Riis publishes "How the Other Half Lives," an 18-page article with photos of life in New York's slums
1890	Stanford White designed his iconic Madison Square Garden
1892	Washington Square Arch designed by Stanford White
	Columbia University moves to Morningside Heights
1897	Park opens at corner of Worth and Baxter streets, ending Five Points slums
1898	Five boroughs consolidated to become New York City
1901	Last cast-iron building constructed at 550 Broadway

1904	IRT subway opens
1906	Stanford White killed
1914	Whitney Museum born with a show at the McDougal Alley
1927	Port Authority buys freight terminal on Hudson River
1929	Stock market crashes
1933	Robert Moses becomes Parks' Commissioner
1951	Jack Kerouac writes iconic beat novel *On the Road*
1952	United Nations establishes Manhattan headquarters
1957	*On the Road* published; Village beatnik scene explodes
1965	Landmarks Preservation Society founded
1968	Paula Cooper opens first Soho gallery
1971	City establishes Department of Cultural Affairs; Artist in Residence program begins
1975	The city nears bankruptcy
1978	Soho's cast iron buildings named National Historic Landmark
1980	Donald Trump revives the Commodore Hotel, opens the Grand Hyatt New York
1990s	Art galleries flock to Chelsea
1992	MTV premiers *The Real World* from a Soho loft
2000	Sugar Hill declared a Historic District
2001	September 11 terrorist attacks
2008	Stock market crashes, leading to economic crisis
2009	The High Line opens

KEY FOR MAP

Current Location

Site no longer exists

M Metro Stop

CHAPTER 1

GEORGE WASHINGTON SLEPT HERE

WHEN NEW YORK WAS THE CAPITAL OF AMERICA

America didn't gain its freedom from the British crown until October 19, 1781, when Lord Charles Cornwallis finally surrendered to George Washington's army after a five-day siege at Yorktown, Virginia. At that moment, almost all of New York City's landowners and merchants were British Loyalists patriotic to King George III. Roughly fifteen thousand of those Loyalists fled Manhattan, leaving their property behind, when American troops finally reoccupied the city on November 25, 1783. For decades, New Yorkers celebrated this date as Evacuation Day.

Of course, New York was a different place back then: The entire city consisted of a few hundred acres around Wall Street. Brooklyn was a far-off county, and properties as near as Gramercy Park were considered country estates.

‹ George Washington bids farewell to his officers at Fraunces Tavern, 1783

City Streets

Pearl Street, originally known as Mother-of-Pearl Street due to all the irides-cent shells embedded in its soil, follows an irregular path today because it once wound its way around the foot of a large hill. As Manhattan's popula-tion grew during the 1700s, new land was retrieved from the East River by leveling those hills, literally creating a street from the water: Water Street. By the mid-1780s, enough land had been moved in front of Water Street to pave yet another road along the waterfront, called Front Street.

The powerful DeLancey family controlled a massive parcel of that land, and maintained their loyalties to the king; James DeLancey was appointed New York's Chief Justice, to the displeasure of many New York colonists, while his father Etienne DeLancey, an enormously successful merchant, maintained the spacious family residence on Pearl Street at Broad Street. Before the defeat of Yorktown, the U.S. Congress declared all properties held by the British crown and its Loyalists to be forfeited. When Cornwallis sur-rendered, those lands were confiscated and sold. The obstinate DeLanceys, who had relied on a British victory to save their real estate dynasty, fell from power dramatically, forfeiting all the land from the Bowery to the East River, from Houston Street down to Division Street. Over a mile of waterfront property was sold to fifteen leading families (the Roosevelts, Livingstons, and Beekmans among them), while the remaining parcels—each the size of one block—were sold to another one hundred and seventy-five purchasers. As the British were driven from New York, the city's streets were promptly renamed: Crown Street became Liberty Street, King Street became Pine Street, Queen Street became Cedar Street. All that remains of the DeLanc-eys' reigning clout is a street with their name on the Lower East Side that even the triumphant colonists were too sentimental to change.

Washington Sleeps in New York

Thanks to its central location, the DeLanceys' home was converted into the Queen's Head Tavern in 1763, later renamed the Fraunces Tavern for its proprietor Samuel Fraunces. (Restored by the Sons of the Revolution, it now stands as a public landmark at 54 Pearl Street.) It was here that General George Washington chose to bid farewell to his troops on December 4, 1783, before returning to Mount Vernon, his family home on the Potomac.

However, in 1785, the U.S. Congress moved to New York. City Hall, as the classically designed building on the corner of Wall Street at Broad Street was then known, became Federal Hall, serving as the first home of the U.S. Congress following the ratification of the Constitution. It was on the steps of Federal Hall, on Wall Street, that the first President of the United States delivered the first Inauguration Address on April 30, 1789, an emotional event marked by thunderous ovations from an enormous crowd.

With New York then the nation's capital, George Washington became one of Manhattan's most celebrated residents. But the leader of the nation's new government needed a home in the capital city. Samuel Osgood, whom Washington appointed to be the first Postmaster General, rented out his house at 3 Cherry Street to be the first Presidential Mansion, for 900 pounds a year. It was instantly known as The Palace, although the building was only three stories high. Not far from today's City Hall, the building was demolished to become the western foundation of the Brooklyn Bridge.

Its use as the Presidential Mansion was problematic, for Washington's stature was quite literal. Standing well over six feet tall, he was among the tallest men in America. The modest construction on the East River had ceilings that were too low, and it was, in the opinion of many New Yorkers, a location too far "out of town" to befit America's first President. So Washington moved. The second Executive Mansion was the McComb house at 39 Broadway, close to Federal Hall, a more fashionable Manhattan address. One year later, the U.S. Congress relocated to Philadelphia and George Washington left New York, never to return.

^ George Washington's first Presidential Mansion, known as
The Palace, at 3 Cherry Street

^ Taverns were the main place for socializing, posting notices and sharing news in early New York

Taverns and Townhouses

Mass confusion defined New York City in the aftermath of the Revolutionary War. Loyalists raced out, soldiers returned home, and shrewd Americans seized confiscated properties at bargain prices. Locating friends and relatives was a daunting task. Churches and taverns were the main places to share news and post notices, and the most likely places to locate acquaintances.

At the Merchants' Coffee House, where dice and backgammon were played amidst the celebrations of General Washington's victorious troops, a radical idea was hatched: a registry. All New Yorkers were encouraged to list their names and addresses, permanent or temporary, which allowed returning friends and relatives to find them. Everyone in New York, it seems, made their way to the Merchants' Coffee House to participate in the inaugural registration process. After assembling data for three years, the city's first directory was published in 1786. (A year

earlier, Philadelphia published a similar directory—the first in the New World.)

According to the first directory, nearly every block had a tavern. Of the 3,340 buildings in New York City, 330 held licenses permitting the sale of liquor. A tavern license cost 30 shillings (New York's currency was measured by pounds and shillings well into the nineteenth century), from which the Mayor and City Clerk each kept six shillings; the rest went to the city's treasury.

Very few original residential buildings still stand. Instantly recognizable by their pointed roofs, a row of early houses from 1796 was moved and restored on Harrison Street at Greenwich Street, where they exist now as privately owned residences with modern interiors. The exteriors of these landmark townhouses, however, are cherished examples of New York's earliest residential architecture.

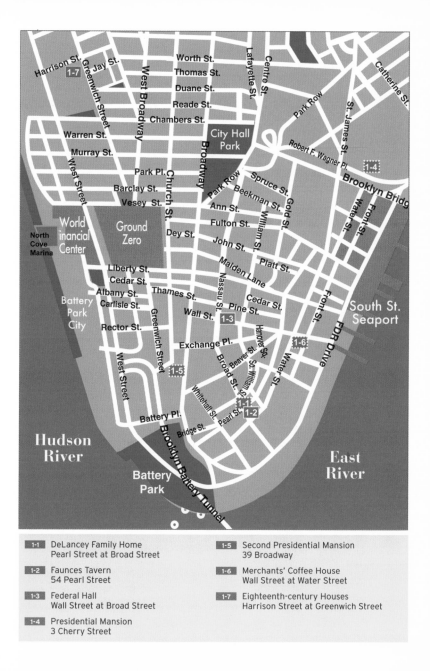

1-1	DeLancey Family Home Pearl Street at Broad Street		**1-5**	Second Presidential Mansion 39 Broadway
1-2	Faunces Tavern 54 Pearl Street		**1-6**	Merchants' Coffee House Wall Street at Water Street
1-3	Federal Hall Wall Street at Broad Street		**1-7**	Eighteenth-century Houses Harrison Street at Greenwich Street
1-4	Presidential Mansion 3 Cherry Street			

CHAPTER 2.

DRUNK ON WATER

AARON BURR'S PROFITABLE GAMBLE

"Don't drink the water!" had to be one of the perpetual cries from the Dutch settlers who founded New Amsterdam. In fact, those Dutch settlers were so parched during their first summer that they almost gave up and moved away. Things didn't improve quickly: For nearly two hundred years, New York's water was so putrid even horses wouldn't drink it, and drunkenness couldn't be reprimanded since so many people had to mix spirits with their water just to swallow it.

Meanwhile, the solid bedrock which provides remarkable support for today's skyscrapers made drilling practically impossible for seventeenth-century settlers with primitive tools. The water they tapped underground was usually rainwater that seeped through the soil, contaminated along the way by all manners of impurities, and collected in depressions above the granite hulk that defines the island of Manhattan. One of the preferred pumps for

‹ **[top]** The Tea Water Pump Garden provided drinkable water from a spring on what is now Park Row. **[bottom]** The Croton Reservoir drinking water was located just outside the walls of Trinity Church, where rainwater was distributed after passing through hundreds of decomposing corpses in Trinity's graveyard.

The only decent, potable water came from a spring on what is now Park Row, between Baxter and Mulberry Streets. A pump was placed over this spring and water for tea was sold to those who could afford it. Ornamental grounds were laid out around the pump, which became known as the Tea Water Pump Garden, one of Manhattan's first parks. The well was four feet in diameter and twenty feet deep. The Tea Water Pump was operated by an enormous handle that only the burliest men could manipulate. Its water cost 3 pence for one hundred and thirty gallons at the pump, or 1 cent per gallon delivered to your door. "Tea Water Men" drove around Manhattan, selling water from heavy casks.

Corruption was inevitable. Tea Water was the only drinkable water in town, but was controlled by a group of thugs who made outrageous profits and whose wagons, waiting their turn to pass under the pump, blocked traffic for a mile in all directions. Something had to be done about the water situation.

In the fifteen years following the Revolutionary War, many individuals approached the Common Council with proposals to improve the water supply, but not until two thousand New Yorkers died in an outbreak of yellow fever did the Council finally take action. They approved an idea presented by the unscrupulous politician Aaron Burr. He proposed the installation of wooden pipes leading from the pond adjacent to the Tea Water Pump, which would provide running water to subscribers for $20 per year, an astronomical sum at the time.

Burr then maneuvered a bill through the State Legislature that granted a charter to The Manhattan Company, his private waterworks. It also included a cunning provision: The water company could use its "surplus capital in any manner not inconsistent with the constitution and laws of this State." On April 11, 1799, with Aaron Burr as Chairman of the Board, The Manhattan Company entered the waterworks business. A mere four months later, The Manhattan Company took their "surplus capital" and opened a bank. With capital stock of $2 million, the bank began operations at 40 Wall Street. Years later, the Manhattan Company became Chase Manhattan, the third largest retail bank in America during the twenty-first century.

Like a growing organism, New York City pushed its roots down into the earth: Thousands of logs were bored, laborers dug up the streets of Lower Manhattan, and new wooden pipes were buried five feet underground, two feet from the curb. With the main artery running down Broadway, The Manhattan Company laid six miles of wooden plumbing in its first year, providing water to four hundred families. While the bank prospered, the waterworks were a constant nuisance.

Without meters, subscribers could run the water all they wanted. Non-subscribing friends were invited to take their fill from those who felt they paid too dearly for the poor-tasting water. Merchants gave it away for free to their steady customers. The wooden pipes proved to be impractical, as they were constantly lodged with debris. Subscribers often went for weeks without water, while the Manhattan Company tore up the streets to locate a clogged pipe and clear it, causing endless traffic jams. (Yes, Manhattan even had traffic jams in 1800.)

The Manhattan Company eventually laid twenty-five miles of wooden pipes, supplying water to two thousand families, far short of its original plan. Although they tried, the company couldn't sell or lease its water rights without also losing its banking privileges. For forty more years, The Manhattan Company half-heartedly provided water to New Yorkers, while its bank flourished. Most New Yorkers chose to collect rainwater in backyard cisterns for free.

In 1832, contaminated water spread cholera, killing thirty-five hundred New Yorkers. Finally admitting that Manhattan's wells and ponds were hopelessly polluted, the Common Council asked the voters to approve a dam on the Croton River in Westchester County, which would provide fresh water via an

^ Aaron Burr, 1802

aqueduct into Manhattan. When the vote succeeded on April 16, 1835, The Manhattan Company was off the hook, able to concentrate exclusively on banking.

New Yorkers ratified a closed-masonry aqueduct spanning forty-five miles. It led into a fifteen-million-gallon receiving reservoir at 86th Street (now Central Park), which in turn filled the distributing reservoir at Fifth Avenue and 42nd Street (where the New York Public Library is located today). The project cost $12 million and required six years of labor and one hundred and sixty-five miles of plumbing to be laid under the streets of Manhattan. At dawn on June 22, 1842, the valve was opened and Croton River water began to fill the aqueduct. In Manhattan, people waited all day, having no idea of how long it would take for the water to reach them. Twenty-two hours later, at three o'clock the next morning, a cheer arose that lasted until the rushing water drowned it out.

On July 4, 1842, the Croton Distributing Reservoir at 42nd Street officially opened its tanks. Water gushed into the Reservoir while New Yorkers celebrated their fabulous new amenity. The celebrations culminated when the aqueduct finally opened on October 14: church bells rang all day, one hundred cannon blasts signaled the beginning of a five-mile parade and water spouted from fountains, hydrants and hoses. Firemen marched in the streets to the cheers of neighbors; President John Tyler also attended the festivities, along with former Presidents Martin Van Buren and John Quincy Adams. A fountain in City Hall Park gushed fifty feet high. Not only did New York finally have all the water it needed, it even had enough to waste.

New York was changed forever as crystal clear water roared through the conduits. New Yorkers were soon using thirty million gallons a day.

Townhouse construction blossomed as residents gave up their Greenwich Village cisterns for new homes with running water in developing neighborhoods such as Murray Hill, Turtle Bay, and Gramercy Park. Some folks landed on the east side, some headed west. For over a century, those neighborhoods developed the profiles that their proud residents cherish today. You know, it's in the water.

2-1 Trinity Church
74 Trinity Place

2-2 Tea-Water Pump Garden: Park Row
between Baxter and Mulberry streets

2-3 Manhattan Company
40 Wall Street

2-4 Receiving Reservoir
86th Street in Central Park

2-5 Distributing Reservoir
Fifth Avenue at 42nd Street

2-6 City Hall Park

CHAPTER 3

EARLY BOHEMIA

THE ROOTS OF GREENWICH VILLAGE

In 1789, when New York was America's capital, President George Washington lived a short distance from Federal Hall. Vice President John Adams, on the other hand, resided in a suburb called Greenwich Village.

Eighteenth-century Greenwich Village looked little like the fashionable neighborhood it is today. As Adams' wife, Abigail wrote: "In front of the house, the noble Hudson rolls his majestic waves." In fact, the Hudson River lapped up on a narrow sandy beach called Hudson Street, where the Adams children swam and fished. Minetta Brook emptied into a swamp between Charlton and Houston streets. It was a pastoral scene of verdant fields and woodlands—but not for long.

Because of its high ground, Greenwich Village was considered a healthful area for summer homes, away from the noise and filth around Wall Street. When cholera, smallpox, and yellow fever turned "all streets below City Hall" into an "infected district" in 1822, thousands of New Yorkers evacu-

‹ A poster advertising the Kiralfy family, one of many dance acts popular in the bawdy clubs of Frenchtown and Bleecker Street ated to Greenwich Village to avoid the plague. The Village limits soon expanded as hills were flattened to accommodate transit, creating new streets to the west, and filling in the marshes to the east.

Adams' mansion, known as Richmond Hill, later became the home of Senator Aaron Burr. The humiliation that followed the tragic duel in which Burr killed Alexander Hamilton was a profitable opportunity for John Jacob Astor, the early real estate investor. To appease Burr's creditors, Astor foreclosed on the famous mansion, moved it to a flatter area down the street, then turned it into a tavern and a resort, later a series of theaters. Pastoral Greenwich Village was beginning to get raucous.

On nearby 3rd and 4th streets, French immigrants opened the saloons of "Frenchtown." Meanwhile, black girls danced in next-to-nothing at the Black and Tan Concert Hall on Bleecker Street and Scotch Ann's was a brothel where whores were young men with painted faces and women's names.

^ Richmond Hill, home of John Adams and, later, Aaron Burr

Cozy cafés tucked away on winding streets attracted scores of writers, poets, actors, and intellectuals, who called themselves "bohemians" as they sought to maintain the lifestyles they once enjoyed in Paris. Walt Whitman patronized Pfaff's, his favorite beer hall at Broadway and Bleecker Street, where enthusiasts clustered to hear him read and speak. Essayist Ralph Waldo Emerson, who advocated anti-slavery and Transcendentalism among other new ideas, sniffed that the boisterous environment was strictly for "noisy and rowdy firemen." (Firemen were low-paid workers who shoveled coal to keep furnaces ablaze, not New York's Bravest, who fight fires.) Nonetheless, it was soon fashionable for denizens of other neighborhoods to venture to Greenwich Village for an evening of observing the bohemians with their curious behavior and colorful dress.

With little effort, bohemians turned Greenwich Village into one of New York's most entertaining districts, reaping a fortune for Astor, who sold almost sixty-two acres of the old Adams land to speculative builders. Many of the Federal townhouses within today's Charlton-King-Vandam Historic District were built by speculators who acquired their land from the Astors.

With its innocence lost, Greenwich Village provided another kind of diversion: collective rage. In 1837, New York University erected a Gothic Revival building on the northeast corner of the parade grounds at Washington Square, constructed from stones cut by convicts at Sing Sing, the maximum-security prison located about thirty miles up the river in Ossining, New York. The indignant stonecutters of New York's Stonecutters Guild promptly organized New York's first mass labor demonstration in Washington Square, which continued for days. To complete its construction, NYU was forced to call in the 27th Regiment of the National Guard to clear the demonstrators from the site.

It became clear that a diverse crowd could be addressed when any cause was proclaimed loudly enough within Washington Square. To the east, the lofty eyes of academia (New York University, to this day, remains the largest private educational institution in the United States), while

^ The fatal duel between Aaron Burr and Alexander Hamilton, 1804

on the north side, protestors could shout to the wealthy inhabitants that occupied magnificent townhouses. To the south, the bawdy proletariat of Frenchtown was always reliable when it came to radical causes, and to the west, the densest population of laborers in America.

Washington Square was suddenly the epicenter of Greenwich Village, a focal point for America and an ideal gathering place for the exercise of free speech. For more than a century, Washington Square has vigorously hosted Civil War riots, women's suffrage demonstrations, labor union rallies, racial equality rallies, teachers strikes, anti-war protests, draft card burnings, flag burnings, bra burnings, love-ins, smoke-ins, and gay rights demonstrations—the list goes on.

Today, Greenwich Village is one of the largest historic districts in the nation: its architecture is protected by landmark status. Far from musty, the Village continues to identify with its radical, bohemian past; its free-thinking ambience is kept alive by young and old, rich and poor, gay and straight residents all living together side-by-side.

Somewhere, John Adams is smiling.

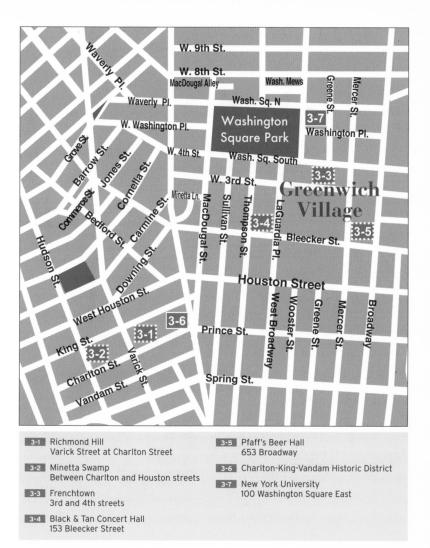

3-1 Richmond Hill Varick Street at Charlton Street	**3-5** Pfaff's Beer Hall 653 Broadway
3-2 Minetta Swamp Between Charlton and Houston streets	**3-6** Charlton-King-Vandam Historic District
3-3 Frenchtown 3rd and 4th streets	**3-7** New York University 100 Washington Square East
3-4 Black & Tan Concert Hall 153 Bleecker Street	

CHAPTER 4

FIFTH AVENUE'S FIRST BREATH

A POTTER'S FIELD BECOMES WASHINGTON SQUARE PARK

Two hundred years ago, New York City smelled. Water was putrid. Garbage festered in mud. America's second-largest city—only Philadelphia was larger—was no longer a neat little Dutch village: Nearly a hundred thousand New Yorkers squeezed into just seventeen thousand low-rise buildings below Canal Street. With no urban plan to shape the unhealthy neighborhood, merchants dwelled above shops and families lived among warehouses and rowdy saloons.

As yellow fever regularly swept through town, yellow shrouds marked the bodies of those who succumbed to the disease. The bodies of the poor were buried in a nine-acre municipal square about two miles north of the settlement, amidst farmland. Today, that nine-acre potter's field is Washington Square Park, the beginning of Fifth Avenue, an international symbol of fashion and wealth.

‹ The original wooden arch in Washington Square, 1889

Fifth Avenue was born in 1807, when New York's aldermen agreed to implement an urban plan. Three commissioners spent four years surveying Manhattan's hills and orchards while speculators tried to buy up land ahead of them; landowners set dogs on them, pelted them with vegetables, and then filed the first lawsuits against the city. Eventually, those commissioners devised Manhattan's grid of one hundred and fifty-five streets and sixteen avenues. According to the urban plan, the municipal square would serve as the base for the fifth avenue.

From its very inception, Fifth Avenue was special. It was an elegant hundred-foot-wide boulevard for strolling, created decades before Baron Haussmann transformed Paris with its Champs-Élysées, and it provided a healthy escape from the downtown miasma. The grid plan was an early urban planning success. None of the great European capitals could boast of such efficient and disciplined use of real estate. As lots within the grid were sold, builders, residents, and services followed in logical succession, and a new city emerged from the soil.

The stretch of Fifth Avenue from the burial ground to 13th Street was opened in 1824: its land was graded and the street was paved. Cobblestones were too uneven, so city planners settled on larger Belgian blocks abutted tightly together. The curbstones—not native to the New World—were milled in England; they served as the ballast on British ships that docked regularly. Since all vehicles had iron-rimmed wheels, traffic noise roared like thunder.

The marsh at today's Washington Square became the public gallows. When the Marquis de Lafayette visited in 1824, he was treated to the sight of twenty highwaymen hanged by the neck. In 1826, the city stopped burying bodies in the square, planted some trees, paved some paths, and officially opened the Washington Military Parade Grounds on July 4, 1828, in honor of the first President. But the park occasionally offered reminders of its less-than-aristocratic past when, as one Washington Square resident wrote, "the weight of heavy guns drawn over the Parade Ground crushed the tops of some of the coffins," exposing the rotted corpses below.

Although it is estimated that twenty-five thousand bodies were decomposing beneath it, the city fathers selected Washington Square as the place to install the large well from which all Fifth Avenue residents would acquire their water. Even more amazing, those neighbors praised the water for its "clarity and softness."

With the newly organized city grid, well-heeled New Yorkers suddenly found it desirable to live apart from shops, warehouses, and saloons. Manhattan's wealthiest residents built the first Fifth Avenue houses and those along the north side of Washington Square.

The Rhinelander family, for example, had lived in New York since the 1600s as importers of china and glass, then sugar. In 1840 William Rhinelander built 14 Washington Square North at the corner of Fifth Avenue; his relatives moved into number 17. Their presence attracted other well-to-do New Yorkers, including James Lenox, who built a manse at 53 Fifth Avenue (at 12th Street). Although rich, these families lived in comfort rather than luxury, for it was fashionable to be "careful with money."

However, both families were soon speculating in New York City real estate to great success—their legacies live on in Lenox Hill and the landmark Rhinelander Mansion on Madison Avenue, now Ralph Lauren's headquar-

^ Parades along Fifth Avenue celebrate the centennial of George
  Washington's inauguration, April 1889

ters. The families of rich businessmen soon populated all the lots "in the Fifth Avenue", with gardens in the front yard and privies in the back.

Life seemed idyllic—magnificent houses on a street with twenty-foot sidewalks, rich friends, relatives, a park, and a water source nearby. With all the shops and businesses two miles downtown, New Yorkers suddenly needed a mode of transportation. The next arrival on Fifth Avenue: stagecoaches. Even well-to-do families chose not to own a carriage, to avoid the costs of a full-time coachman, horse, and stable. Instead, starting in 1830, coaches—with six people on either side—roared up and down the avenue, and Second, Third, Sixth, and Eighth avenues as well, charging a nickel a ride. As one citizen put it: "...nowhere in America were so many fine horses to be seen. Formal coaches with high springs and double-folding steps. Indeed, Fifth Avenue was akin to a horse show."

Street life required street lamps. Gas lines were laid underground, starting in 1825. By 1847, street lamps extended all the way to 18th Street, maintained by lamplighters who switched the valves on each night with the tip of a long wand.

Next came education. When New York University opened on Washington Square East in 1831, the nearby residents were its chief donors. In the halls of higher learning, sons of those early residents were groomed to run the world. One such son, John Taylor Johnson became an executive at the New Jersey Central Railroad, ran an art gallery, and then founded the Metropolitan Museum of Art.

Education inspired invention. Samuel Morse invented the telegraph while serving as a professor at NYU. Soon telegraph wires were strewn from giant poles throughout the city, as communication with the downtown offices took on a new immediacy. Wealthy Fifth Avenue residents installed buzzers in their houses to summon "telegraph boys" to pick up messages. The area's bucolic atmosphere began to fade as commerce encroached.

Churches followed the money, regularly relocating when residential neighborhoods turned commercial. They observed that as their congregations shrank with the influx of commerce, real estate values increased. Churches reaped profits by selling real estate (usually to be razed) in a burgeoning market, and then followed their congregants to new neighborhoods. On Sundays, churches were permitted to put chains across Fifth Avenue during services to prevent noisy stagecoaches from disrupting solemn worship.

Then Delmonico's, New York's premier restaurant, moved from William Street up to Fifth Avenue and 14th Street, bringing new excitement with it. Lower Fifth Avenue was now called the "social spine of New York" and its glory days would last from the 1830s through the 1880s. "Promenading" became a male sport. Young men, attired in the very best London-made fashions, strutted with high hats, turned-up cuffs, and canes. Meanwhile, Mercer Street, just three blocks from elite Washington Square, was the main promenade for streetwalkers, with nearby taverns supporting a surprising number of brothels.

In April 1889, the city celebrated the centennial of George Washington's inauguration, with a parade ending at a triumphal wooden arch spanning Fifth Avenue, just one hundred feet north of the square. New Yorkers from all neighborhoods were so dazzled by the temporary edifice that a permanent marble arch was installed in Washington Square to meet public demand. The completed arch was inaugurated in May 1892, commemorating the four hundredth anniversary of America's discovery. It was the same year that cornerstone was laid for the Cathedral of Saint John the Divine on Amsterdam Avenue at 112th Street, and just five years before Columbia University moved from 49th Street at Madison Avenue to Morningside Heights.

As the successful grid-city became as vibrant as the rowdy area below Canal Street, New Yorkers began to settle further and further uptown. Observing the popularity of their neighborhood—a parade route, bohemians flocking to nearby Greenwich Village, and bawdy shows on Eighth and Bleecker

^ By 1893, stagecoaches are a familiar sight on Fifth Avenue, as seen in this drawing from *Harper's Magazine* streets—the Fifth Avenue elite admitted the unthinkable: again, their neighborhood had begun to smell.

Turning up their noses, these stylish New Yorkers continued the city's uptown expansion.

4-1	Washington Military Parade Grounds
4-2	Rheinlander Homes 14 Washington Square North 17 Washington Square North
4-3	Lenox Home 53 Fifth Avenue at 12th Street
4-4	New York University 100 Washington Square East
4-5	Delmonico's Fifth Avenue at 14th Street

Fifth Avenue Style

Easter Sunday on Fifth Avenue, ca. 1890, by W.T. Smedley

An afternoon lounge at Goupil's Art Gallery, Fifth Avenue and 22nd Street, 1872, in *Leslie's Illustrated Newspaper*

Ladies' drawing room in the Fifth Avenue Hotel, 1859, in *Harper's Weekly*

CHAPTER 5

FROM DYNASTY TO TRAGEDY

THE STORY OF THE ASTOR FAMILY

Few people believed as strongly in the viability of New York as John Jacob Astor. Barely two years after Cornwallis surrendered to George Washington, Astor immigrated to Manhattan in 1783 at the age of twenty, uneducated and barely fluent in English. With him he brought $25, seven German-made wooden flutes, and a wily sense of opportunism.

The son of a butcher from Waldorf, Germany, Astor started out in New York by peddling cakes in the streets for a bakery on what is now Cedar Street. When a nearby resident offered him a job at the rate of $2 a week in the fur trade, young Astor headed up the Hudson River to Iroquois country, carrying a rifle and a sixty-pound backpack. He played his wooden flute as he traveled, often twenty miles a day, to negotiate with trappers and Indians for precious pelts, and defending his blonde scalp from hostile tribesmen. In his first year, Astor not only developed contacts in the fur trade, but also learned to navigate the forests, and identify America's natural resources better than most merchants.

‹ Mrs. Astor greets guests at her exclusive ball, 1903

He skillfully applied that knowledge. Profits on fur pelts were enormous, especially in Europe, where prices escalated as the American Revolution disrupted the trapping industry, causing a scarcity of pelts. Astor continued his forays into the profitable Niagara frontier, sleeping under the stars. In 1785, he married his Queen (now Pearl) Street neighbor Sarah Todd, presenting her with the seven flutes. Sarah's $300 dowry was used to import European instruments and establish her in the music business, with the front room of the Todd house (81 Queen Street) functioning as a showroom. In 1789, just five years after arriving in America, Astor retired from the musical instrument business, applying its capital to two lots on the Bowery, purchased for $625 cash. Over the next six decades, while his fur business prospered with employees across America, Astor found his greatest source of income: Manhattan real estate.

Accurately assuming that European immigration would escalate, he avoided the purchase of properties already developed, preferring farmlands he could divide into numerous lots, for great profit. To them Astor applied the European concept of twenty-one-year leases, after which the property plus the tenants' improvements reverted back to him. With famine and political hardships throughout Europe, Manhattan was a boomtown. By the time Astor died in 1848, Manhattan's population increased from twenty-five thousand residents in 1785 to five hundred fifteen thousand. With a frantic need for more housing, Manhattan development progressed further uptown and Astor—who owned much of the bare land upon which new homes were erected—earned the title of New York's Landlord.

With his wealth came power, which he managed from his office at 71 Liberty Street and his home at 223 Broadway, near Vesey Street. Astor held the mortgage for the Greenwich Village estate of Governor DeWitt Clinton, a $75,000 investment that eventually generated $1 million annually for the Astor heirs. He even duped President Thomas Jefferson by circumventing the Embargo Act, allegedly returning a "Chinese mandarin" to his homeland on one of Astor's trade ships. When the boat returned to America loaded with rare teas, Astor sold his goods on the American market for $200,000, his largest transaction yet. He then used the profits to acquire all the land from Broadway to the Hudson River, from 42nd to 46th streets.

But he wanted even more. Seeking an aristocratic title within his family, Astor arranged the marriage of his daughter Eliza to a Swiss Count. He was subsequently presented to Charles X and Louis Phillippe of France, met with Prince Metternich, and attended the coronation of Ferdinand II.

Despite his conspicuous wealth, Astor was a famous miser, generous only within his family. On one of his many return visits to Waldorf, Germany, he traveled in steerage to save a few dollars. Once in Germany, however, he pensioned every relative he could locate. In New York, where one in seven residents was a pauper, he gave away nickels to children begging in the streets. When an Episcopal minister chided that Astor's philanthropy was out of scale with its potential, he switched to dimes.

In 1834, Astor built the most luxurious hotel on this continent, eventually known as Astor House. He moved his residence "uptown" to the west side of Broadway at Prince Street, sharing a business office with his son William at 85 Prince Street, and also maintaining a thirteen-acre "country estate" at Hell Gate, today's 88th Street and Second Avenue, where he entertained some of the greatest intellectuals of the era.

He befriended Aaron Burr (while also holding Burr's mortgage), Martin Van Buren, Daniel Webster, and Washington Irving, whom he regaled with stories of his colorful past. At their urging, Astor's philanthropy finally materialized in his later years. Appreciating the importance of learning, he created a library for the public at Astor Place, investing $60,000 in "curious, rare, and beautiful books." While he didn't live to see Astor Library's completion—he died in 1848, just one year before it opened—he bequeathed $400,000 toward the library building's maintenance. Today the books belong to the New York Public Library, and the building has since been reborn as the Public Theater.

^ John Jacob Astor

Between 1820 and 1850, property values in Manhattan rose from $83 million to $286 million, of which almost $30 million belonged solely to John Jacob Astor, a staggering sum in pre-Civil War America. Responsible for much of Manhattan's earliest real estate development, the enterprising Astor rendered an unforgettable legacy, but he could not foresee the impact his great wealth would have on his heirs.

With New York City real estate investments providing steady income, Astor's grandson William Backhouse Astor Jr. inherited the bulk of the fortune by accepting his family's plan for an arranged marriage. His bride, Caroline Webster Schermerhorn, was no great beauty, but her family had lived in New York far longer than any Astor, a pedigree the family sought with vigor. Although the marriage seemed ideal to the twenty-two-year-old Caroline, twenty-three-year-old William only hung around long enough to sire four daughters and a son, but then concentrated his efforts on his millionaire playboy lifestyle. Traveling on an enormous yacht, he spent much of his time away from his family.

Mrs. Astor had other plans. With four daughters to marry off, she was determined to identify suitable partners for each of her children. In 1872, she met Ward McAllister, a Southern gentleman fascinated by New York society. Working with Mrs. Astor, who provided the money and the organizational skills, McAllister conceived the idea of a ball committee. Twenty-five

^ The Astor House hotel, Broadway between Vesey and Barclay streets

prominent men—including Schermerhorns, Astors, and, of course, McAllister himself—invited five men and four ladies to every party. They became the patriarchs of New York society, controlling the very definition of who and what was fashionable.

Local publications and many tongues soon referred to Mrs. Astor as "Society's Queen" or the "Mystic Rose," dubbing McAllister as her "Prime Minister." Once their list of invitees had been established, the Balls were subscription affairs attended by the same celebrants at each gathering. Catholics and Jews were never invited to the Astor Balls. Neither were the Vanderbilts, nor the "nouveau-riche" Goulds and Harrimans. Trading on such obvious exclusions, the select list of invitees made the affairs an instant success.

As McAllister later wrote: "Applications poured in from all sides; every influence was brought to bear ... Pressures were so great that we feared the struggle would be too fierce and engender too much rancor and bad feeling." To save face, a second string of parties, known as the Family Circle Dancing Class, was arranged to pacify the disgruntled, and included a younger set, to whom the Astor daughters might soon debut.

The renowned events took on legendary proportions. Each January, Mrs. Astor gave a ball at the family's mansion at 350 Fifth Avenue (at 34th Street). Bedecked in a fortune of jewels and posing under a life-size portrait of herself, Mrs. Astor greeted her guests alone.

As her daughters neared their debuts, McAllister and Mrs. Astor increased the attendance of the balls to four hundred. While Mrs. Astor explained that it was the maximum number that her ballroom could comfortably accommodate, McAllister audaciously told the press: "Why, there are only about four hundred people in fashionable New York society. If you go outside that number you strike people who are either not at ease in a ballroom or else make other people not at ease."

Presenting the Astor children to the New York 400 was a triumph, and the ballroom soon served as the site of family nuptials. In 1876, Emily Astor married James Van Alen, a dashing Civil War cavalry commander and an investor in the New York Central Railroad. In 1878, Helen Schermerhorn Astor married James Roosevelt Roosevelt, confirming ties with the powerful Roosevelt family. Soon after, Orme Wilson married Carrie Astor, with his family providing a $400,000 marriage settlement, and a distinguished guest list that included former President Ulysses S. Grant—wedding gifts reached a value of about $1 million.

Only Charlotte Astor surprised all society (and, inevitably, the press), after her marriage to James Coleman Drayton. Ten years into her marriage, and as the mother of four children, she fell in love with Hallett Alsot Borrowe, the vice president of Equitable Life, left her family and ran off to Europe with her lover. Even from his yacht in Florida, Charlotte's father William Astor was scandalized. He retaliated by writing her out of his will (although mother Caroline, who outlived her husband, made provisions to care for Charlotte years later).

That left only son John Jacob Astor IV to find his partner in society. A lavish reception for eight hundred guests introduced him triumphantly in 1887. John Jacob IV married the most gentried spouse of all: Ava Lowle Willing, a descendant of Alfred the Great, Henry I, Edward I, Henry III, and Henry IV of England, and Henry I of France. (Sadly, it was this same John Jacob Astor who died on the Titanic in 1912.)

Mrs. Astor had accomplished her task, confirming the Astors as one of the most powerful families in New York, while establishing the standards by which all of society's fêtes have been measured since.

The Astor family's reputation as keepers of society lasted through the twentieth century, led by Brooke Astor, the widow of John Jacob Astor's great-grandson Vincent. The last of the Manhattan Astors, Brooke Astor died in 2007 at the age of one hundred and five. A leading social figure and philanthropist, her final years were filled with illness and mental deterioration, along with rumors of abuse and neglect at the hands of her son (from a previous marriage), Anthony Marshall.

In 2009, eighty-five-year-old Marshall was found guilty of grand larceny, having siphoned tens of millions of dollars from his mother's estate. He was sentenced to prison for up to three years, a sad end to a glittering chapter in Manhattan history.

5-1 Astor's First Job Cedar Street bakery	**5-6** Astors Move "Uptown" 585 Broadway
5-2 Todd House 81 Queen (Pearl) Street	**5-7** Office of John Jacob & William Astor: 85 Prince Street
5-3 Astor Office 71 Liberty Street	**5-8** Astor Country Estate 88th Street at York Avenue
5-4 Astor Home (later the Astor House Hotel): Broadway between Vesey and Barclay streets	**5-9** Astor Library (Public Theater) 425 Lafayette Street
5-5 Astor's Big Buy Broadway to the Hudson, from 42nd to 46th streets	**5-10** William B. Astor Mansion 350 Fifth Avenue

CHAPTER 6

A BEAR ON BROADWAY, AND A RIOT AT THE OPERA

A BRIEF HISTORY OF ASTOR PLACE

When the Commissioners' Plan successfully leveled all the hills and valleys in Manhattan in 1811, urban agriculture ended. Farms were replaced by row-house developments along the patterned grid of streets and avenues we know today. The expense and disruption to property owners provoked some of New York's first acts of civil disobedience, at a time when Manhattan was as wild as the West.

Broadway and the Bowery, two important commercial streets already in use, were to be extended uptown, following their existing courses. Those extensions would cross, forming a natural union at 11th Street, creating a Union Square. Hendrick Brevoort, a sixty-four-year-old descendant of early Dutch settlers, lived in the wooden house his father built on 11th Street at the Bowery. He had no intention of partitioning his land or parting with his splendid grove of trees. Learning of the planners' determination to raze the trees to make way for 11th Street, Brevoort acquired a "pet" bear, which he kept chained to a tree. Guarding his land with a blunderbuss firearm while

‹ At least twenty-five were killed during the May 10, 1849 riot at the Astor Place Opera House the bear protected the other side, Brevoort defied the Commissioners' Plan.

To this day, 11th Street meets a dead-end at Broadway, where Brevoort's grove once thrived. To avoid any altercations with Brevoort or his bear, the commissioners revised their plans for Broadway. At 10th Street, it would run parallel to the Bowery, giving us a Union Square at 14th Street, where the Bowery (now Fourth Avenue) and Broadway never meet.

When Brevoort died in 1841 at age ninety-four, his son Henry sold the grove to the Grace Church for $35,000. The trees were razed two years later by Brevoort's nephew James Renwick, a twenty-five-year-old aspiring architect who had not yet designed a single project. With Grace Church as his first commission, Renwick's career and reputation were launched, culminating in his magnificent design for Saint Patrick's Cathedral a decade later.

^ [top] James Renwick [bottom] Hendrick Brevoort's farm at the junction of Broadway and the Bowery, 1831

Meanwhile, the elegant home of William Backhouse Astor's family stood nearby on Lafayette Place. Around the corner stood the eighteen hundred-seat Astor Place Opera House. When an American actor, Edwin Forrest, received favorable notices for his performances on London stages, some high-minded New Yorkers thought it wise to produce *Macbeth* at the Astor Place Opera House, inviting Forrest's longtime British rival William Macready to perform. Theatergoers were furious. With wounds from the War of 1812 still too fresh in the minds of many New York veterans, Macready's appearance was a chance to fight one more battle with the British.

On May 10, 1849, an estimated crowd of twenty thousand gathered in front of the theater, while three hundred policemen escorted ticketholders inside.

^ Grace Church, located on Broadway at East 11th Street

When Macready entered onstage as Macbeth, the theater erupted with hoots, jeers, and flying vegetables. The mob outside hurled cobblestones at the Opera House, shattering the front windows of the theater. Inside, ringleaders threw cobblestones at the theater's huge chandelier. Cut glass rained down on the audience. Meanwhile, the mob outside attacked the police. By 10 p.m., the National Guard arrived, but when guardsmen shot their firearms overhead to avoid bloodshed, the mob reached a wilder frenzy, attacking the National Guard head-on. The Colonel gave the guard orders to fire at will.

From their residence, the Astors saw the National Guard fire directly into the mob. Their theater was in shambles. The melee finally ended at 1 a.m., when the guardsmen moved two brass cannons into position. The cannons weren't used; as the sun rose, two hundred protestors were wounded, and thirty-four lay dead in the street.

6-1 Brevoort Farm
11th Street and Bowery

6-2 Union Square

6-3 Grace Church
802 Broadway

6-4 Astor Place Opera House
425 Lafayette St

6-5 The Colonnade
William B. Astor's Residence
428-434 Lafayette Street

Views of New York

View of New York from the Hobuck Ferry House, 1800, by Francis Jukes

New York, 1851, printed by Goupil & Co.

New York with Brooklyn Bridge, after 1883

CHAPTER 7.

SLUMMING

THE STORY OF FIVE POINTS

New Yorkers love to describe their city in superlatives: the biggest population, the tallest buildings, the richest millionaires, even the winning-est baseball team. What you rarely hear is the converse, though it too is true. When it comes to squalor, historic Manhattan just can't be beat, for it fostered the sleaziest, dirtiest, sickest slum in American history, just a short walk from City Hall.

The notorious slum was called Five Points. Today it only exists in the movies, most notably in Martin Scorsese's *Gangs of New York*. It's the area that partially comprises today's vibrant Chinatown, though the streets of Five Points are long gone. Imagine the era before running water, before paved streets, decades before Lincoln freed the slaves. Imagine an era when people considered it "proper" to segregate themselves by gender, by race, by religion and ethnicity. Now imagine a place where poverty is so severe that it blurs all those divisions, shocking all of "respectable" society. That was Five Points, a neighborhood packed with people desperate to survive within the wooden buildings that lined the foul and muddy streets.

‹ Bottle Alley and Bandit's Roost (left), were two infamous alleyways in Mulberry Bend, the most dangerous neighborhood in all of New York, and the subject of the 1890 book *How the Other Half Lives* by Jacob Riis

The place earned its name from the five corners created by several intersecting streets (where today's Worth and Baxter streets intersect, west of Mulberry Street), though the neighborhood spread for blocks in all directions. There was once a pond there, Collect Pond, and it was the neighborhood's primary attraction, since water was a rare commodity on this island of solid bedrock.

When some two-and-a-half story buildings were erected near the pond a neighborhood was born. Those half-stories were usually workshops, as in the early 1800s most Americans worked with their hands. Enterprising locals became saloonkeepers; there were saloons on every block in Five Points, serving as sources for news as well as camaraderie. The unskilled laborers—many of them African-Americans who escaped slavery in the South—unloaded cargo ships in the harbor, or broke rocks to clear the land.

The area declined rapidly. American cities lacked the zoning laws we take for granted today and in the Five Points, residences, shops, and industries stood side-by-side. Pigs and sheep were corralled through the streets and into the local slaughterhouses; their skins were sold to tanneries. The pond that provided fresh water for residents of Five Points was the same pond where tanneries, breweries and slaughterhouses dumped their waste. The pond eventually became so putrid and polluted that a ditch was dug just to drain it; Canal Street was born when the pond was filled with land.

With no pond, landlords added wells and cisterns to the yards behind the tenements, far too close to their outhouses. As more immigrants crowded into the tiny rooms of Five Points, outhouses continually contaminated the water supply. As a result, cholera was a chronic illness. The stench was chronic too, but even educated people didn't make the connection. Most residents outside of Five Points simply viewed cholera as a natural condition of the "degraded" lowlifes living there. Doctors were scarce and frequently mistrusted. Residents relied on the saloons to provide their water, mixing spirits in it just to make it drinkable.

The destitution led to an unbelievable spectacle. Since there wasn't sufficient work for the rapidly increasing population, everyone learned to be a huckster of some sort, selling a service to make one day's pay stretch for a week. Prostitution was rampant; thanks to its central location, Five Points became the most popular red-light district in New York.

The Old Brewery, the neighborhood's largest and most notorious building, was converted into tiny tenement rooms. Pickpockets roamed the dark hallways and thieves stashed their booty in the windowless spaces; elsewhere, dozens of people of all races would sleep in a pile on each other for warmth.

The small wooden buildings were just as bad: walls were pasted over with newspapers to keep out the elements, yet landlords had no incentive to demolish these decrepit buildings, for the taxes on an old building were a fraction of what they'd pay on a new one, yet the tenancy would remain the same. Drunken brawls were a daily occurrence, spilling out into the unpaved streets. The sober ones placed bets on which drunk might prevail.

The spectacle was too enticing. In 1834, the *New York Sun* published sensational exposés, reporting "the drunkards of both sexes, intermingled with scarcely any thing to hide their nakedness, lay in a state of misery almost indescribable." That same year, Davy Crockett, Tennessee's famous frontiersman, arrived for a visit and published his observations: "Black and white, white and black, all hugemsnug together with a jug of liquor between them: and I do think I saw more drunk folks, men and women, that day, than I ever saw before." He concludes: "I would rather risque myself in an Indian fight than venture among these creatures after night ... these are worse than

^ The Old Brewery in the Five Points, 1852

savages, they are too mean to swab hell's kitchen." Davy Crockett's publication offered up the Five Points' notoriety to a national audience.

In 1841, British author Charles Dickens took a swipe at the Five Points, too, writing in his *American Notes*: "Here, too, are lanes and alleys, paved with mud knee deep; underground chambers, where they dance and game; hideous tenements which take their name from robbery and murder; all that is loathsome, drooping and decaying is here." Dickens' visit was a cue to fashionable New Yorkers to go "slumming." With a police escort, wealthy visitors would arrive to gawk at the poverty on display and marvel at the vices of its residents.

Meanwhile, famine in Ireland sent extraordinary numbers of starving immigrants to America. Five Points was the inexpensive place for housing, where resourceful landlords divided wooden buildings into smaller and smaller "tenant apartments," or "tenements" for short.

Next came the Southerners, sneering that Five Points justified slavery. As one Kentucky doctor put it, Five Points' cholera patients "are far more filthy,

^ The intersection of Cross, Anthony, and Orange streets, 1827 degraded, and wretched than any slave I have beheld, under the most cruel and tyrannical master." The *Southern Quarterly Review* mused: "is [there] any negro quarter, from Mason and Dixon's line to the Rio del Norte, which could furnish a picture of vice, brutality, and degradation comparable to that drawn from the Five Points of New York?" It seemed that everyone came to judge, but few offered solutions.

The city government occasionally sprayed the streets and buildings with disinfectants, but did little to resolve the source of the misery. Elected officials heard from temperance societies, missionaries, reformers and other do-gooders, but no one agreed on what should be done to end the wretchedness in the Five Points. When the Civil War ended and slaves were freed, African-Americans arrived in New York only to face a new kind of discrimination. While many black men learned such skills as carpentry or masonry while working in the South, those jobs were off-limits in New York. Instead, black men shoveled coal and took other menial jobs to survive; Five Points was one of the few places in which they could afford to live. It became the most densely populated neighborhood in the world, with three hundred and

^ Policemen lead upper-class tourists through the Five Points slum, 1885 thirty-five thousand people per square mile circa 1888.

Right about then, the squabbling and squalor reached an abrupt end, thanks to the efforts of one lone man with a remarkable new gadget. Jacob Riis was a Danish immigrant who arrived in New York in 1870. Living a true rags-to-riches life, Riis dwelled in poorhouses, sold flatirons, and eventually landed a job as a reporter for the *New York Tribune*. For eleven years, he covered the Five Points beat, writing the brutal stories of its mean streets. Riis was also one of the first reporters to get his hands on the earliest flash attachment for a camera. It changed his career and the map of New York.

Riis left the *Tribune* in 1889 to write an eighteen-page article for *Scribner's Magazine* that included nineteen of his photographs, which were coarse, heartbreaking evidence of the lives behind the dilapidated buildings. Here were starving children in windowless rooms, looking straight into the flash of a camera. The article, famously entitled *How The Other Half Lives*, was a national sensation. Slumming lost its charm.

Next, Riis took his show on the road. He made lantern slides of his photographs, then spoke at churches and lecture halls with W. L. Craig from the Health Department. Together they articulated what no one had figured out: cholera and other diseases were not genetic afflictions of the poor. Diseases were chronic throughout Five Points because of polluted drinking water and the lack of sanitation.

^ Jacob Riis, 1890

Riis continued to photograph with the flash. He expanded *How The Other Half Lives* into an entire book, published in 1890. In it he delivered hard-hitting statistics such as the shocking infant mortality rate on Mulberry Street in 1888: a whopping sixty-eight percent. These harsh realities stunned the nation. Theodore Roosevelt, then head of the New York Police Board of Commissioners, arrived at Riis's office with a note that simply said: "I have read your book, and I am here to help." Riis took Roosevelt on a series of nighttime tours. Soon after, Roosevelt closed the broken-down lodging rooms, and added his voice to Riis' in a call to replace the Five Points' tenements.

The park at the corner of Worth Street and Baxter Street, the former Five Points intersection, opened on June 15, 1897, and is still a playground today. Although it lacks the spacious charms of Central Park, it represented a gargantuan step by city government to acknowledge the importance of light and air when designing an urban environment. Entire streets were erased as New York reinvented the Five Points neighborhood by razing its buildings and leveling the land.

A few years later, Theodore Roosevelt, as America's twenty-sixth President, praised Jacob Riis as "the most useful citizen of New York." In that moment, he proved that in Manhattan even sad stories can end in superlatives.

^ Three boys sleep in the street in this photograph by Jacob Riis, 1888

From Five Points to Chinatown

Chinese people didn't find their way to America in large numbers until the California Gold Rush in 1849, and many worked their way across the country on the Transcontinental Railroad. With the completion of the railroad in 1869, thirty thousand men were put out of work; America's prosperity was threatened. New laws flagrantly discriminated against the Chinese: ineligible for citizenship, forbidden to marry Americans, forbidden to defend themselves in courts, even denied bail. Most hurtful of all, the U.S. Congress enacted the Chinese Exclusion Act in 1882, prohibiting all immigration from China. Women were prevented from joining their husbands, and by 1900, less than five percent of New York's Chinese population was female. "Chinese must go!" was proclaimed by politicians from all parties, while anti-Chinese legislation remained in effect until 1943.

During those sad decades, Chinese men across America were subjected to stonings, burnings, beatings, and riots that ended in murders. Union officials labeled Chinese immigrants as "the greatest danger to organized labor in America" since Chinese laborers were often hired just to cross picket lines. To escape to a safe haven, Chinese men migrated to two American cities that were famous for their tolerance: San Francisco and New York.

When the Exclusion Act became law in 1882, desperate Chinese men made Five Points their new home, the melting pot, at last. Generations of Irish immigrants who once populated the place were now inching their way into the middle class and out of the poor neighborhood. Chinese bachelors took their place.

From the cruel treatment they'd experienced elsewhere in America, these Chinese men realized that to live safely in America, they needed to be self-sufficient. Two types of businesses flourished: laundries and restaurants. In these industries, no one could claim that Chinese laborers were taking work away from American citizens. That's how Chinatown was born.

Today, Manhattan's Chinatown is still famous for its proliferation of restaurants, but the cultural mix is changing. While its earliest Chinese settlers were primarily Cantonese, new dialects are taking over Chinatown as immigrants arrive from other provinces, finding comfort in familiar sounds and smells.

Meanwhile, the neighborhood is undergoing yet another transformation, as a new wave of restaurants, boutiques, and art galleries bring a youthful energy to this old-school New York neighborhood.

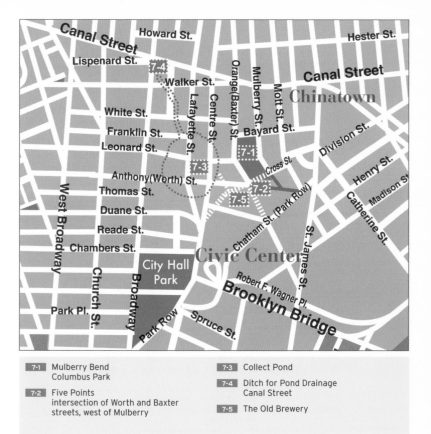

7-1	Mulberry Bend Columbus Park	**7-3**	Collect Pond
7-2	Five Points intersection of Worth and Baxter streets, west of Mulberry	**7-4**	Ditch for Pond Drainage Canal Street
		7-5	The Old Brewery

CHAPTER 8.

MANHATTAN'S INCANDESCENCE

THOMAS EDISON ELECTRIFIES NEW YORK

Inventor Thomas Edison invited New York City's aldermen to his New Jersey laboratory on January 2, 1880, served them champagne and a catered feast, then proudly presented his latest invention: the incandescent lamp. Here was steady, brilliant illumination, a major improvement over gaslight's irregularly flickering flames. The aldermen balked.

Thrilled by his own ingenuity, Edison recommended that city funds be spent to string electric wires throughout Manhattan, placing his new invention on every street corner. The aldermen groaned: Sure, the light bulb was an impressive gimmick, but why give up New York's beautiful gaslights? Corruption was legendary, and politicians regularly sold their allegiances to the highest bidder. Since the mayor firmly backed the gas companies, the aldermen viewed Edison with caution. Manhattan's skyline was already marred

< The operating room at Edison Station, 1896

by drooping telegraph wires, telephone wires, and stock tickers, which the Board of Aldermen now used against Edison to intentionally hamper his progress. They passed a law prohibiting him from installing electrical wires overhead anywhere in New York. Their message to Edison was plain: Don't mess with the gas companies. Instead, the city continued to pay a small army of lamplighters fifty cents a month for each lamp they maintained, with each route including up to one hundred lamps per night.

Unfazed, Edison displayed his light bulb to private users. He recognized, two years earlier, that if he was to perfect an electric light bulb, he would need control of the electrical source first. With J.P. Morgan's investment bank handling the finances, he formed the Edison Electric Light Company, selling shares to New York's most prominent industrialists, including railroad tycoon W. H. Vanderbilt, Western Union director Hamilton Twombley, and others.

J. P. Morgan was among the richest men in New York and he saw the potential impact of Edison's bold new gadget, and the windfall that would surely accompany it. When Morgan retained Edison's company to install electric lights throughout his home at 219 Madison Avenue (at 36th Street), the race was on. While there are no written records as to what swayed the aldermen, on April 19, 1881, over the objections of the mayor, but with the muscle of Morgan and the Vanderbilts, Edison was granted official use of one square mile of Lower Manhattan's streets for the purpose of installing underground electrical conduits.

Following J. P. Morgan's endorsement, investors clamored for the new lighting systems. Edison bought 255-257 Pearl Street for $150,000, installed six electrical generators, and began the costly process of digging up Manhattan's unpaved streets and embedding the conduits that would one day carry electricity.

He opened a school at 65 Fifth Avenue, where The New School currently stands, to teach his employees about electricity. Meanwhile, the suspicious Commissioner of Public Works, another friend of the gas lobby, assigned five fulltime inspectors to observe the labors of Edison's installers, demanding that Edison pay each of them the exorbitant salary of $5 per day. (In 1881, many New Yorkers were earning $5 for a 60-hour work week.)

With not a single bulb in operation, investors still flocked to Edison. By opening new electrical companies in several neighborhoods, Edison sold shares of stock to meet the growing demands of additional investors. By October 1, 1881, he had strung wires into the buildings of fifty-nine customers. His stock, which had a face value of $100, soared, sometimes advancing by $100 an hour. It rose to $500, then $5,000, then $8,000.

Finally on September 4, 1882, thirty-five-year-old Edison invited investors, scientists, and journalists to J.P. Morgan's opulent bank at 23 Wall Street to watch the lights come on. It was chief electrical engineer John Lieb who put the massive Pearl Street generators in motion just before 3 p.m. Tension rose as the assembled guests alternately watched the unlit lamps, the emotional Edison, and the hands of the clock as they swept toward three. A minute before 3 p.m., one of Morgan's directors cried out: "A hundred dollars the lights don't go on."

^ Thomas Alva Edison, 1878

"Taken!" Edison shouted back. Then he turned the switch, bringing all one hundred and six lights in Morgan's office to life in one historic gesture. That same day, electricity was delivered to eighty-five Manhattan addresses wired with four hundred light bulbs, including some prominent shops on Nassau Street, and fifty-two lamps in the editorial room of the *New York Times* at 41 Park Row. As dusk descended, Manhattan was illuminated. A *Times* article described the noteworthy product the following day: "The light was more brilliant than gas and a hundred times steadier ... with no nauseous smell, no flicker, no glare."

Within fourteen months, Edison's companies provided service to five hundred and eight subscribers with twelve thousand seven hundred and thirty-two bulbs. The need for his product was immediately apparent, to the collective dismay of the mayor, the aldermen, the employees and shareholders of New York's six gas companies. For decades, whenever a light bulb burned out, a technician from Thomas Edison's company was summoned to the site to perform the scientific task of changing a light bulb, and it was well into the twentieth century before all of New York was wired for electricity.

Edison announced his goal, to "make electric light so cheap that only the rich will be able to burn candles." In the process, Edison's remarkable achievements gave birth to two companies that today's New Yorkers know well. The light bulb manufacturing company became General Electric in 1883. The electric companies Edison established in various neighborhoods were eventually merged into one entity: Consolidated Edison, today's Con Ed, the original mass provider of electricity.

^ The Madison Avenue home of J.P. Morgan, the first New York residence wired for electricity

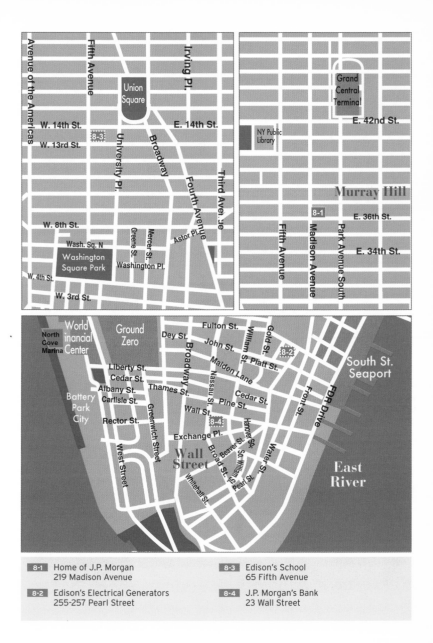

8-1 Home of J.P. Morgan
219 Madison Avenue

8-2 Edison's Electrical Generators
255-257 Pearl Street

8-3 Edison's School
65 Fifth Avenue

8-4 J.P. Morgan's Bank
23 Wall Street

CHAPTER 9

FROM DEUTAL COVE TO COVETED ADDRESS

THE EVOLUTION OF TURTLE BAY

Some Manhattan neighborhoods seem to coalesce spontaneously: Soho, Noho, West Chelsea, and TriBeCa grew in response to Manhattan's tight housing market, their dwellings created within commercial facades. Meanwhile, other neighborhoods have been residential since before New York City was a city.

Consider Turtle Bay—the area defined roughly as 43rd Street to 53th Street, between Lexington Avenue to the East River. This bay was actually a marsh that formed a cove between East 41st to 48th streets, the present site of the United Nations. Water trickled into it from a spring at the southeast corner of today's Central Park. The cove proved useful to seafaring vessels during the Revolutionary War in 1776, and to Robert Fulton, who tested his steam-powered boats there in 1808. But by the 1860s, the bay was covered with landfill.

Where are the turtles? Not in Turtle Bay, surprisingly. The area earned its name when, in 1639, the Dutch governor of New Amsterdam permitted two

‹ James Beekman, 1761

Englishmen to settle there after they were captured. The original land grant referred to the property as "Deutal," the Dutch word for a bent blade, in reference to the shape of the land. In 1664, when the British captured New Amsterdam, "Deutal Bay" was anglicized into Turtle Bay, the name it's had ever since.

The land was divided into two farms. To the south, Turtle Bay Farm was owned by Sir Peter Warren, a British Naval Officer who was later buried with honors in Westminster Abbey. His neighbor to the north was James Beekman, a notorious Revolutionary patriot who built a mansion near 51st Street and First Avenue, which he named Mount Pleasant. The British occupied this mansion during the Revolutionary War, using its greenhouse for the trial and sentencing of patriot Nathan Hale in 1776. One day later, near the Dove Tavern at Third Avenue and 66th Street, Hale uttered his famous last words: "I only regret that I have but one life to lose for my country."

While the two farms were divided into blocks and lots in 1830, Beekman's high ground overlooking the river remained an estate. His nephew, James W. Beekman, became a distinguished New York state senator who developed the property by grading the streets and adding water mains to attract new neighbors, including Horace Greeley, publisher of the *New York Tribune*, who bought seven acres between 48th and 49th streets.

^ The Beekman house at 50th Street and First Avenue

Conversely, Sir Peter Warren's daughters developed Turtle Bay Farm more haphazardly, without restricting the land along the river to residential use; carpentry shops, match factories and breweries filled the dead-end streets. Squatters built shanties at East 42nd Street and a foul-smelling slaughterhouse became First Avenue's prominent new fixture.

Residences were developed in earnest following the Civil War, with brownstones soon lining most streets. After standing for over one hundred years, Mount Pleasant was torn down in 1874, although parts of the house and its furnishings are preserved by the New-York Historical Society. Horse cars on Second and Third avenues caused such congestion that the former property lines of the Beekman and Turtle Bay farms were forgotten. A new kind of divider had arrived: the elevated railway.

The Third Avenue Railroad line opened in 1878 and the Second Avenue line opened in 1880. Although they provided vital communication and rapid transit to a booming city, these railroads compromised Turtle Bay. Sunshine on the wide boulevards was blocked by shadow, and marred by soot and noise, the dingy avenues were filled by pawnshops, bars, and cheap apartments. The proud brownstones to the east of the train tracks became an ever more secluded neighborhood.

By 1900, deterioration overtook those eastside brownstones. Many were divided into inexpensive rooming houses for transient tenants. Throngs of European immigrants subdivided Turtle Bay into ethnic neighborhoods: Italians to the east of Second Avenue, Irish and Germans to the west, while 49th to 51st streets were largely Jewish. East 48th Street became home to transient actors, musicians, and stagehands. By the end of the First World War, Turtle Bay meant low rent.

In 1919, the townhouses of Turtle Bay were "rediscovered". Mrs. Walton Martin envisioned a group of townhouses surrounding a communal garden as she had seen in Italy. She assembled twenty contiguous houses; ten on 49th Street and ten behind them on 48th Street, then reconfigured the adjacent gardens to include a central path and common garden, including a fountain like the one at Villa de Medici in Florence. Following their renovations, the exciting new attraction of "Turtle Bay Gardens" brought attention and revitalization to the entire vicinity.

Powerful residents moved in, including Katharine Hepburn, Tyrone Power, Ruth Gordon and Garson Kanin, Mary Martin, and Leopold Stokowski. Avenue A was renamed Sutton Place, in honor of Effingham B. Sutton, a neighborhood merchant during the 1880s. Soon Beekman Place, Sutton Place, and the adjacent blocks underwent restorations as well, through the efforts of J. P. Morgan's daughter Anne, Theodore Roosevelt's son Kermit, and Mrs. William K. Vanderbilt.

Next came developers with even grander dreams. Fred French planned a "city within a city" for Turtle Bay. In just thirty-five days, he purchased all the buildings between First and Second Avenue, from 40th to 43rd streets, a five-acre assemblage that cost him $7.5 million. In 1928, he opened "Tudor City", twelve magnificent new buildings housing seventy-five hundred people. It brought the neighborhood its own post office, monthly magazine, and landscaped park. Its architects succeeded in blocking the offensive odors from the First Avenue slaughterhouses by facing all living rooms to the West, with back corridors overlooking the river.

The Second Avenue Railroad was torn down between 1940 and 1942. In 1955, the Third Avenue Railroad was demolished, returning Second and Third avenues to cleanliness and light. Once the neighborhood gasped fresh air, it promptly erupted with celebrity. In elegant apartment houses like One Beekman Place and the restored townhouses nearby, Greta Garbo, Cole Porter, Ethel Barrymore, Billy Rose, Lillian Gish, Irving Berlin, Henry Luce, Efrem Zimbalist, Dame Judith Anderson, and other prominent New Yorkers proudly made Turtle Bay their home. In 1946, John D. Rockefeller, Jr. added more luster to Turtle Bay when he acquired all the riverfront property from

^ The Third Avenue Railroad, which ran until 1955

42nd to 48th Street—including the pungent slaughterhouses and breweries—by paying $8.5 million to developer William Zeckendorf. When the U.S. Congress passed a special statute exempting the Rockefellers from gift tax, all property and waterfront rights were conveyed to build the United Nations.

Today, Turtle Bay's past lives side-by-side with modern development. In 2001 Donald Trump opened his World Tower on First Avenue; its 72 stories reach the height of a 90-story building. With Trump's bold statement, the landfill over "Deutal" cove began its next lofty chapter.

9-1 Beekman mansion, Mount Pleasant 51st Street at First Ave	**9-4** Sutton Place
	9-5 Tudor City
9-2 Shanties of Corcoran's Roost First Avenue and 42nd Street	**9-6** One Beekman Palce
9-3 Turtle Bay Gardens	**9-7** United Nations
	9-8 Trump World Tower

CHAPTER 10.

THE GOLD COAST

FIFTH AVENUE MOVES UPTOWN

As soon as the first blocks of Fifth Avenue were paved from Washington Square to 13th Street in 1824, Manhattan's wealthiest businessmen built splendid new homes for their families, escaping the mud and disease of Lower Manhattan. But they faced a big surprise, for their new neighborhood wasn't bucolic for long. The cluster of prominent names within those few streets drew attention to the important new address, forever defining Fifth Avenue by its occupants' wealth.

Meanwhile, down on Beaver Street in 1827, two Swiss brothers opened Manhattan's trendiest restaurant: Delmonico's, soon the most popular French restaurant in New York. Learning the addresses of their wealthiest patrons, the Delmonico brothers attempted a radical move in 1861: They left lower Manhattan to relocate right on Fifth Avenue itself, at the northeast corner of 14th Street, just beyond the famed residences. Delmonico's grand new ad-

‹ Fifth Avenue at 39th Street, 1889

dress bestowed instant prestige; its ballrooms and dining rooms were the scenes of countless gatherings of wealth and fashion. Samuel Morse, the inventor of Morse code and a professor at nearby New York University, even telegraphed the first intercontinental cablegram from his table in Delmonico's grand ballroom.

Prestige was conferred outdoors too, as large-scale projects gained public acceptance when displayed on Fifth Avenue. Gaslights soon lined the sidewalks all the way past 50th Street. Stagecoaches roared up and down the two-way avenue in four-minute intervals. In 1842, the city's massive aqueducts were completed, finally pumping millions of gallons of fresh water into the Croton Reservoir at Fifth Avenue and 42nd Street, where the water was distributed directly into the expensive townhouses down Fifth Avenue. Decorated like an Egyptian temple, the reservoir was an important destination for a Sunday stroll, as visitors climbed its stairs to a forty-foot summit, then strolled around the perimeter. As Edgar Allan Poe wrote in the *Broadway Journal*, "You can see from this elevation the whole city to the Battery, with a large portion of the harbor and long reaches of the Hudson and East Rivers."

With Delmonico's commercial precedent on Fifth Avenue at 14th Street, other businesses eagerly catered to Manhattan aristocrats on their home turf. The blocks between 14th Street to 23rd Street attracted hotels, clubs, and businesses as the avenue expanded northward. Foreign royalty arrived to experience Fifth Avenue, too. The Fifth Avenue Hotel, at 23rd Street, hosted such visitors as the Prince of Wales, the Prince of Siam, Prince Napoleon, and the last emperor of Brazil. It's where politicians conceived their plans to make a president of Ulysses S. Grant and a vice president of Theodore Roosevelt; where celebrities like Mark Twain, former president Chester A. Arthur, and actor Edwin Booth made their New York homes. Nearby, the Victoria Hotel became President Grover Cleveland's New York home between his terms in office, at 27th Street.

The foreign press was impressed too. When it came to wonders like hot running water indoors, British reporter Edward Dicey gushed in 1863, "All the domestic arrangements are wonderfully perfect." However, when reviewing the celebrated residents of Fifth Avenue, they sneered. In London, Anthony Trollope wrote: "I know no great man, no celebrated statesman who has lived on Fifth Avenue. That gentleman on the right made a million dollars by inventing a shirt collar; the one on the left electrified the world by a lotion. Such are the aristocracy of Fifth Avenue."

To proud Fifth Avenue millionaires, there was only one solution: build bigger. If the accomplishments of America's millionaires couldn't earn them acceptance among the old money crowd overseas, then they would dazzle the world by flaunting even greater wealth than crowned royalty. Comforted by American ingenuity and spectacular wealth, the Fifth Avenue gentry knew how to surpass the luxurious lifestyles of those titled Europeans. Pouring their fortunes from private industries into Manhattan real estate, they speculated on the building boom throughout the city, as boatloads of people arrived each day to live in New York.

^ Fifth Avenue south from 27th Street, 1906

Then came the Gold Coast: extraordinary mansions in the middle of America's most urban city, filled with the latest amenities and the best European antiques that Americans could ship back home. Once-sedate residents of lower Fifth Avenue embraced grand new lifestyles, vaunting their wealth through the magnificent facades of homes they built farther up the avenue.

They faced hurdles, too. Who would want to live within the commercial stretch between 14th and 23rd streets? Not Mrs. William Backhouse Astor, for example, who shunned lower Fifth Avenue to establish a house uptown at 34th Street. Other great names soon built grand homes north of 23rd Street.

The Delmonico brothers heard the warning cry and knew it was time to move their operation yet again. If their wealthiest patrons were moving across 23rd Street, so would they. In 1876, Delmonico's lavish new restaurant opened at 26th Street. It soon faced another hurdle: a wild new dessert called ice cream was the rage, and Louis Sherry's restaurant on Fifth Avenue at 37th Street was the best place to find it. Competition was everywhere, in Fifth Avenue's businesses as well as residences.

No one was content with last year's opulence, moving further uptown into more elaborate structures. To residents, this guaranteed good seats at the

^ Delmonico's, 1903

opera, membership in exclusive men's clubs, which also abandoned their roots below 23rd Street, and of course, the best tables at the best restaurants.

So, the Vanderbilts left Washington Square for a new house on Fifth Avenue at 51st Street. Even P. T. Barnum built a residence beyond the reservoir at 438 Fifth Avenue. Fifth Avenue businesses followed their wealthy patrons. When Sherry's Hotel moved to Fifth Avenue at 44th Street, champagne flowed as the celebrated clientele packed the place. Delmonico's faced down their competition by relocating directly across the street. Together, they prospered until Prohibition shut them both down.

The next generation of Vanderbilts erected a mansion at 57th Street, then scored the ultimate coup—a royal title—when their daughter married a European Count. Meanwhile, as the result of a family feud, Mrs. Astor built a mansion at 65th Street, facing the new Central Park. (The feud also resulted in a pair of competing hotels, The Waldorf and the Astoria, on the sites where two Astor mansions once stood at Fifth Avenue and 34th Street.)

And so it went. Developing Fifth Avenue became a fierce Monopoly game. In an era when the average worker earned $12 for a sixty-hour workweek, New York's capitalists and entrepreneurs demolished million-dollar homes and built them again uptown to impress the neighbors.

^ Dinner celebrating the 70th birthday of Mark Twain (second from left), Delmonico's, 1905

The Gold Coast Today

Later generations of New York's wealthiest families sold the choice sites of their childhood homes to reap even greater profits from apartment house construction. However, thanks to philanthropic efforts, several remarkable Gold Coast mansions from this era survive today.

 Henry Clay Frick once controlled the largest coke and steel operation in the world. Carrère and Hastings designed his house at One East 70th Street, which now holds the revered Frick Collection.

James B. Duke's family earned its fortune on tobacco, building several Fifth Avenue residences. His daughter Doris Duke gave their final mansion at One East 78th Street to New York University for its Institute of Fine Arts.

 The Whitney family earned a fortune from railroads and Standard Oil. Their former residence at 972 Fifth Avenue near 79th Street now houses the Cultural Services of the French Embassy.

The final home of Mrs. Cornelius Vanderbilt III was designed by Carrére and Hastings. It stands at the southeast corner of 86th Street and Fifth Avenue, and is occupied today by the Neue Galerie Museum for German and Austrian Art.

 Andrew Carnegie invested his legendary wealth from the Pennsylvania Railroad and steel mills into a mansion so grand that passersby soon called the entire vicinity Carnegie Hill in deference to his imposing residence. It stood at 2 East 91st Street, where the Cooper-Hewitt, National Design Museum of the Smithsonian Institution now resides.

F-1 Henry Clay Frick Residence (Frick Collection) One East 70th Street	**F-4** Cornelius Vanderbilt III Residence (Neue Galerie) 86th Street at Fifth Avenue
F-2 James B Duke Residence (Institute of Fine Arts) One East 78th Street	**F-5** Andrew Carnegie Residence (Cooper-Hewitt Museum) 2 East 91st Street
F-3 Whitney Residence (Cultural Services of the French Embassy) 972 Fifth Avenue	

10-1 Delmonico's (1862)
One East 14th Street

10-2 Croton Reservoir (1842)
Fifth Ave at 42nd Street

10-3 Fifth Avenue Hotel (1858)
Fifth Avenue at 23rd Street

10-4 Victoria Hotel (1868)
Fifth Ave at 27th Street

10-5 William B. Astor Jr., Residence (1862)
350 Fifth Avenue at 34th Street

10-6 Delmonico's (1876)
Fifth Avenue at 26th Street

10-7 Louis Sherry's (1890)
Fifth Ave at 37th Street

10-8 William Henry Vanderbilt Mansion
(1882) Fifth Avenue at 51st Street

10-9 P.T. Barnum Mansion (1867)
438 Fifth Avenue

10-10 Tiffany & Co. (1870)
Union Square West at 15th Street

10-11 Tiffany & Co.: Fifth Ave (1905)
409 Fifth Avenue at 37th Street

10-12 Sherry's Hotel (1898)
Fifth Avenue at 44th Street

10-13 Delmonico's (1896)
Fifth Avenue at 44th Street

10-14 Cornelius Vanderbilt II Mansion (1882)
One East 57th Street

10-15 Mrs. Astor's House (1893)
Fifth Avenue at 65th Street

CHAPTER 11

PARK AVENUE

THE FROG PRINCE

There was a time when Park Avenue was known as Fourth Avenue, and it was populated mainly by breweries, factories, and small farms. Its most notable features were the noisy, filthy trains that ran down two tracks at its center, all the way to Prince Street. An unfortunate ridge of stone, the schist into which many of Manhattan's skyscrapers are embedded, put opposing sides of the avenue at uneven elevation through much of upper Manhattan, making real estate development impractical. Railroad entrepreneur Cornelius Vanderbilt provided a few iron walkways above the tracks for pedestrians, but crossing Fourth Avenue in a carriage was simply impossible in much of upper Manhattan.

Meanwhile, Vanderbilt pocketed a fortune. With more than thirty trains, his railroad transported about eight thousand passengers daily. However,

‹ A railway tunnel below Fourth Avenue, 1876

popular sentiment turned against him when two locomotives exploded and burned below 14th Street. Outraged politicians demanded that locomotive power cease within the "populated" areas of the city, triggering a series of legal precedents. For the very first time, American lawmakers contemplated the regulation of privately owned businesses that "affect the public interest," eventually reaching the U.S. Supreme Court. Vanderbilt complied by stopping his locomotives at his 42nd Street depot, hitching horses to his occupied passenger cars, then hauling his customers to their downtown destinations.

Reformers demanded more. Observing that upper Manhattan's expansion was hampered by the railroad, reformers rallied for the trains to be enclosed in sunken tunnels. To Cornelius, two tracks down Fourth Avenue just weren't enough anymore. In 1872, Vanderbilt purchased the craggy promontory along Fourth Avenue for an astonishingly low price, in exchange agreeing to blast the stone, level the grade of the avenue in the process, and bury his four tracks, which would emerge above ground at 97th Street. His $6.5

^ Grand Central Depot, 1900

million project cost almost $75,000 per block. Ironically, a few months later, an unrelated financial panic hit Wall Street, closing the Stock Exchange for ten days. Businesses went bankrupt, men were suddenly out of work, and Cornelius Vanderbilt easily assembled a workforce of twenty-five hundred men, as laborers clamored for employment.

By 1875, the project was complete. The Avenue was now one hundred and forty feet wide, the grandest boulevard in New York, with fifteen-foot sidewalks, and a fifty-six-foot wide center mall providing relief and ventilation from the not-so-grand fumes, filth, and deafening noise from the tunnel below. With the grade now level, once-mercenary Vanderbilt was viewed as a visionary who provided a spectacular service to the city, and residential real estate development became a possibility above 42nd Street, all along Fourth Avenue.

When Vanderbilt died two year later, in 1877, he was recognized for shortening the New York-to-Chicago travel-time from fifty hours to twenty-four, and for establishing mass transit as a reliable form of transportation within New York City.

In March 1888, the City Aldermen agreed to rename the boulevard Park Avenue. It took a while for society's royalty to accept Park Avenue; its development is solely a twentieth-century phenomenon. It wasn't until September 1906, when the trains were electrified—minimizing the noise and reducing the need for ventilation—that the malls of Park Avenue could be landscaped. Today, the Vanderbilt legacy continues on Park Avenue. Saint Bartholomew's Church, located at Park Avenue and 50th Street, boasts a trio of bronze doors designed by Stanford White and dedicated to the Vanderbilts. Like Fifth Avenue, the first important residences to be erected on the new Park Avenue were not the magnificent apartment houses we revere today; they were one-family mansions for wealthy, powerful New Yorkers.

^ Cornelius Vanderbilt

One of the first and most prominent mansions was erected in 1905 at 71st Street, the home of Secretary of State Elihu Root, designed by Carrère and Hastings. The *Real Estate Record* commented that Root "built a handsome house, and the result has been to improve the character and tone of the neighborhood ... which fact alone will make the section a fashionable and restricted quarter for many years to come."

Mansions on Park Avenue

Some terrific mansions still stand on Park Avenue, though their days as private residences appear to be over. Some converts:

680 Park, designed by McKim, Mead & White, was formerly the residence of Percy Pyne, but later became the Soviet Mission to the United Nations. Its second-floor balcony was the site of two much-publicized press conferences held by Premier Nikita Khrushchev in 1962. It was later purchased by a granddaughter of John D. Rockefeller, who donated it to the Center for Inter-American Relations.

686 Park, the former home of William Douglas Sloane, head of the W & J Sloane furniture and carpet stores, was sold in 1959 to become the Italian Cultural Institute.

690 Park, built for Henry Pomeroy Davison, a founder of Bankers Trust, then later a partner of J.P. Morgan, was sold along with 52 East 69th Street in 1955, to become the Italian Consulate.

^ **[top]** The sunken track of the N.Y. and Harlem Railroad, Fourth Avenue, 1876

11-1	Vanderbilt's 42nd Street Train Depot	P-1	Percy Pyne Mansion: 680 Park Avenue (Center for Inter-American Relations)
11-2	Saint Bartholomew's Church 109 East 50th Street	P-2	William Douglas Sloane Mansion: 686 Park Avenue (Italian Cultural Institute)
11-3	Elihu Root's Mansion 733 Park Avenue	P-3	Henry Pomeroy Davison Mansion: 690 Park Avenue (Italian Consulate)

CHAPTER 12

MR. VANDERBILT BUILDS HIS DREAM HOUSE

A MANSION ON MILLIONAIRE'S ROW

When it comes to marvelous Manhattan residences, no modern-day fantasy can measure up to the astonishing reality of post-Civil War New York. During the late nineteenth century, when immense fortunes were being amassed, there was no better means by which to display great wealth and proclaim self-importance than through the public spectacle of a Manhattan mansion. No one, it seems, did it better than the descendents of Cornelius Vanderbilt, who erected no less than four resplendent mansions along Fifth Avenue between 52nd and 57th Street, a stretch soon dubbed "Millionaire's Row."

One such grandson was Cornelius Vanderbilt II. Blessed with a stunning fortune, "Corneil" and his wife Alice observed that fashionable society was moving uptown, away from the 14th Street thoroughfare and the Astor man-

‹ Mrs. Cornelius Vanderbilt dressed as Electric Light, Vanderbilt Ball, 1883 sion at 34th Street. In 1879, at age thirty-eight, Corneil acquired two brown-stones at the corner of Fifth Avenue and 57th Street, then demolished them. He hired George Post, the only architect who was regularly invited to Mrs. Astor's New York 400 balls, to design the Vanderbilt dream house at One West 57th Street.

Inspired by the Chateau de Blois in the Loire Valley of France, built of red bricks and limestone, Post's design for the mansion included turrets, bays, and a huge mansard roof with multiple gables. The sumptuous interior boasted Corneil's important art collection, including works by Henri Rousseau, Jean-Baptiste-Camille Corot, Jacob van Ruisdael, and J. M. W. Turner, among others. He retained John LaFarge, the renowned decorative artist, to create the stained glass windows and sculptured ceilings, while Augustus Saint-Gaudens created the sculptural staircases and Karl Bitter embellished the paneling. Inlays of gold, silver, ivory, and pearls were everywhere. New York's newest mansion was also its most chic private museum. As a monument to the power and achievement of the Vanderbilts, the edifice was an enormous success.

The Vanderbilt mansion heralded the emergence of imperial America. Here was a family lacking royal blood, yet its wealth and prestige rivaled any noble house in Europe. The Vanderbilt mansion confirmed the limitless possibilities of the New World; it captured the imaginations of people everywhere.

From its construction in 1881, the Vanderbilt mansion was a tourist attraction. The passengers of every carriage on Fifth Avenue knew when they were passing the home of Alice and Cornelius Vanderbilt II. Yet those within the Vanderbilts' social circle were less impressed. Montgomery Schuyler in the *Architectural Record* sneered: "A sad botch, incident to a reaching desire after imposing effect." After a few gala social functions, Alice and Corneil had to admit that they too had envisioned something better. Their beautiful first-floor drawing rooms were no substitute for a real ballroom. If they were to entertain on the epic scale that befitted their social prominence, they needed a bigger house.

Back came architect George Post, this time in concert with Richard Morris Hunt, while Louis Tiffany served as interior designer.

Corneil purchased and demolished the four remaining brownstones on Fifth Avenue, then built a new facade that adjoined the manse at 4 West 58th Street, facing Grand Army Plaza and Central Park. While the original mansion cost a staggering $750,000 to construct, the new addition and renovation cost an extra $3 million, as crews worked around the clock, often under giant electric lights. Even with eight hundred laborers, construction took two years. The Vanderbilts got their ballroom, along with a porte cochere (a covered driveway that enabled guests to enter without fear of rain or mud), massive fireplaces, boiseries (finely detailed architectural carvings, sometimes called "gingerbread") and ormolu (molded brass fittings, often applied onto marble). Upon its completion, the Vanderbilt dream house was the largest private residence in America.

However, even among Vanderbilts, dreams don't always manifest themselves according to plan. Eldest son William died of typhoid at age twenty-two, but not before introducing his younger brother Neily to Miss Grace Graham Wilson, a beautiful and worldly debutante. Three years later, when Grace turned up again, on the arm of Neily Vanderbilt, Corneil and Alice recognized the real cost of making a public spectacle of their wealth. They perceived Miss Wilson as a social climber, out to marry a Vanderbilt, any Vanderbilt.

^ The Vanderbilt Mansion at Fifth Avenue and 57th Street, 1908

In Paris, Neily pledged his devotion to Grace, and Corneil traveled to Europe, threatening to exclude Neily from his will.

The press on two continents had a field day following the domestic entanglements of America's richest star-crossed lovers.

In July 1896, Corneil banished Neily from One West 57th Street; days later he was felled by a stroke. All of America wondered if death would again visit the Vanderbilt dream house. With his father on his deathbed, Neily married Grace in her family's mansion at 608 Fifth Avenue in August 1896, which the press reported as the wedding that cost Neily $60 million, since disinheritance seemed inevitable. When Corneil died of a cerebral hemorrhage in 1899, he was only fifty-six years old. True to his word, Corneil's last will, dated on Neily's wedding day, bequeathed $42 million to younger son Alfred, while Neily was given $500,000.

The saddest part came next. Alice inherited the dream house, filled with treasures she and Corneil barely had the chance to enjoy. For twenty-six more years, Alice resided there, seldom entertaining, haunted by her memories. Hotels, shops, offices, and overwhelming noise soon enveloped her now-too-public home. In 1920, the real estate taxes alone cost $130,000; it was time to part with the dream house. That's when Alice faced another crushing reality: no one in twentieth-century America could afford to live like a nineteenth-century Vanderbilt. She waited for years and finally acquiesced to the Braisted Realty Corp., an organization that saw little romance in the dream house. It paid $7.1 million just to get the land and knock it down.

But first, in one last gloriously sentimental gesture, Alice invited the public to tour the house for one week in January 1926. The 50-cent admission fees were donated to charity. Movie theater baron Marcus Loew bought fragments of the house that he installed in various Loew's theaters across America, including the giant Tiffany chandelier from the Moorish room, which went into the foyer of the Loew's State Theater in Syracuse.

^ Cornelius Vanderbilt II with Mayor William Jay Gaynor and Theodore Roosevelt (standing), 1910

In 1927, Fifth Avenue lost one of its most splendid landmarks: Vanderbilt's dream house was razed. The painted ceilings, the mirrored walls, the massive staircases, the carvings, and the mantles were all smashed into rubble and hauled off to a New Jersey landfill. Corneil's daughter Gertrude Whitney, founder of the Whitney Museum, paid to remove the imposing wrought-iron gates, which are now at the entrance of the Conservatory Gardens in Central Park. The Saint-Gaudens fireplace from the entry hall, and some of the glasswork by John LaFarge are all that remain of the interior. You can view them today in the American Wing of the Metropolitan Museum.

12-1 Astor Mansion
Fifth Avenue at 34th Street

12-2 Vanderbilt Dream House
One West 57th Street

12-3 Family Home of Grace Graham
Wilson: 608 Fifth Ave

12-4 Conservatory Gardens in Central Park

12-5 Metropolitan Museum

CHAPTER 13

DOWN THE MIDDLE

CENTRAL PARK, AND HOW IT GOT THAT WAY

"A miracle in the middle of Manhattan!" is the way one tour guide describes Central Park. But the real miracle is that this urban oasis even exists, for the dramatic story of its construction involves classism, racism, cronyism, patronage, politicking, and of course, unscrupulous real estate developers.

In 1851, the idea of a great park was proposed by Mayor Ambrose Kingsland, primarily because city aldermen recognized that the real estate holdings bordering Manhattan's seventeen public squares—which comprised a mere one hundred and sixty-five acres—maintained the greatest value. Therefore, to encourage real estate development north of 42nd Street, a great park was needed. The initial plan detailed that a one hundred-fifty-acre park would be created from 66th to 75th streets, from Third Avenue to the East River. The strongest proponent of that plan was State Senator James William Beekman, the nephew of merchant James Beekman, who owned fifteen acres of land

< Squatter settlements and shantytowns were common in and around
Central Park until about 1885, when they were replaced by more
permanent urban development

just one block south of the proposed park. Beekman could profit mightily from increased real estate values, although he claimed that his primary interest was in enabling "all classes" of New Yorkers to share the "seaside breezes" of the waterfront. In typical New York fashion, dissent was prompt and passionate. Would "all" New Yorkers really benefit from an eastside park? Since most New Yorkers lived below 42nd Street, why was the park funded by general tax revenue, when it would only benefit uptown development?

The Special Committee on Parks recommended in 1852 that the park be constructed from 59th Street to 106th Street, from Fifth Avenue to Eighth Avenue. Recognizing the site's irregular topography—"numerous abrupt and rocky elevations, intersected constantly by ravines and gentle valleys"—made the place impractical for conventional real estate development. As a result, only a few parcels had ever been sold within this area; the state government owned much common land and would not need to purchase the property allocated for the reservoir. When compared with the numerous buy-outs they faced with the landowners of the East Side location, New Yorkers favored the lower per-acre acquisition cost. As it turned out, the aldermen who most virulently defended the site were also some of the first to speculate and profit by purchasing parcels of land adjacent to the proposed park, prior to its official designation.

Before development could begin, a design needed to be created, and the present landowners needed to move. Most of the people who owned land in the craggy marsh were African-Americans, it turned out (although in these years prior to the Civil War, black residents were not yet American voters). Back in 1825, Andrew Williams, a bootblack, bought three lots for $125 near 85th Street on the West side. His friend Epiphany Davis, a trustee on behalf of the African Methodist Episcopal Zion Church, bought twelve lots for $578, designating some of the land to build a church. More black families arrived, developing Seneca Village, a community of modest farms, also known as a safe haven for runaway slaves.

In 1853, park commissioners offered $700 per lot to each landowner, a significant profit, but an end to a burgeoning community. On October 1, 1857, the residents of Seneca Village scattered, quietly and without violence, enabling the construction of Central Park. The African Methodist Episcopal

Zion church disappeared without a trace, although in 1959, a park gardener discovered a human skull, buried in what was once the graveyard of the church.

Meanwhile, a contest was announced: $2,000 would be paid to the designers of the best plan for a seven hundred and seventy-eight-acre park, with the costs not to exceed $1.5 million, about $34 million today. Furthermore, the park required four or more cross streets connecting Fifth to Eighth avenues, a twenty- to forty-acre parade ground for militia drills "with proper arrangements for the convenience of spectators," three playgrounds of up to ten acres each, a prominent fountain, a winter skating lake, and a lookout tower.

Thirty-three designs were submitted, with some courageous ideas: one suggested a massive fresco on the reservoir walls depicting the history of the American Revolution. Several proposals included an exhibition hall, concert hall, or lecture hall. Other proposals included: an open-air stadium for horse races; a one-third mile-long shooting gallery for cannons, muskets and pistols; bath houses for lake swimmers; a collection of Chinese, Norwegian, Italian, and Swiss lodges "to provide interest and variety;" and even a special lawn for women, equipped for gymnastics and archery, protected for privacy by a giant hedge. Some were concerned with issues beyond aesthetics: one called for mounted police and telegraph stations at every gate so that ruffians could be "marked, followed, watched, and annoyed in every way by

^ The Grand Drive, Central Park, 1869

authorities;" another noted that the parade ground should be located away "from those parts on Eighth Avenue where drinking shops will be most likely to locate;" while another advocated that all carriages be banned, enabling New Yorkers of all economic backgrounds to appreciate the park as equals.

The winning entry was announced on April 28, 1858, awarding Calvert Vaux, an English architect, and Frederick Law Olmsted, the park superintendent, the opportunity to enact their vision. Above all, Olmsted and Vaux emphasized rural scenery, "to suggest the pleasant ideas of harmonious proportion, fitness, and agreeable variety to the eye." They also realized that carriages traveling through the park for recreation required different paths than those for "coal carts and butchers carts, dust carts and dung carts." By sinking the transverse roads eight feet beneath the park surface, commercial traffic would never jeopardize "those agreeable sentiments that we should wish the park to inspire." More than one hundred years later, we still praise Olmsted and Vaux for their progressive thinking.

However, the park of today is not the park of Olmsted and Vaux's vision. Almost from the day of its approval, commissioners tinkered with the design, often against the wishes of its designers. For starters, that $1.5 million allocation was woefully insufficient. To reduce costs, two transverse roads were eliminated, as were exterior iron fences, a music hall, and a conservatory. When Olmsted wrote that he was "thoroughly worn out, used up, fatigued beyond recovery," the commissioners advanced him $500 and sent him abroad for six weeks to "examine European parks," while work continued without his scrutiny. By the time of the park's completion in 1866, twenty thousand laborers had moved nearly two and half million cubic yards of stone and earth. With hand tools and gunpowder they had broken through three hundred thousand cubic yards of gneiss rock veined with granite, stacked six million bricks, fertilized the land with forty thousand cubic yards of manure, and planted two hundred seventy thousand trees and shrubs, for the then-exorbitant cost of $5 million (well over $100 million today).

Even before it was finished, Central Park was welcomed with vigorous enthusiasm. To Olmsted and Vaux, that was the ultimate compliment. As

^ Frederick Law Olmsted, 1860

aldermen predicted fifteen years earlier, the new park was a feat that befitted the greatness of the new city. With the stench of the swamp and farm animals a fuzzy memory, the properties flanking the park were now ripe for development. Even before the nine miles of carriage drives were completed, two-thirds of visitors arrived by carriage, confirming the upscale appeal of the properties surrounding the park. Sure enough, on the park's east side, the value of Fifth Avenue land tripled within only five years, as wealthy families built homes in a stretch soon designated as Millionaire's Row. When The Dakota was erected on the West Side, America's first luxury apartment house gave new meaning to "a room with a view"; it served as a model for future apartment houses that were erected on both sides of the park.

Today, no other city in the world can boast such an expanse of greenery at the foot of so many residences in the center of the city. The area's ever-escalating property values might be viewed as an unspoken tribute to the visions of Frederick Law Olmsted and Calvert Vaux.

13-1 Central Park	**13-3** Seneca Village
13-2 Proposed Plan for Central Park 66th to 75th Street from Third Avenue to East River	82nd to 89th Street between Seventh and Eighth avenues
	13-4 The Dakota One West 72nd Street

CHAPTER 14

IT HAPPENED IN GRAMERCY PARK

THE COOPERATIVE GETS A LIFT

The first cooperative apartment house in New York was not on Fifth Avenue, it was at 34 Gramercy Park. The astounding story that precedes its inception reads like a mini-history of New York City, involving a lengthy list of celebrated New Yorkers.

Gramercy is an anglicized version of the Dutch word "crommessie," meaning "a small crooked knife," which referred to the shape of the brook that later flowed through giant conduits placed underground in the 1830s. The crommessie's wild terrain, dropping as much as forty feet in some areas, made farming impractical, but noting the city's booming population, landowner Samuel Ruggles raised a small fortune to move mountains of earth, divert water, and level the landscape to make it habitable. Today's New Yorkers pay plenty for a water view, but in the 1800s a brook simply meant mud, stench, and vermin—a definite detriment to residential development. Ruggles had two radical ideas: to build townhouses around an open square, guaranteeing light and air, and to permit the owners of those houses to maintain the parkland privately, free of government participation. That last

< A crowd gathers around the home of former Governor Samuel J. Tilden, Gramercy Park, 1877

idea was even more slippery than diverting the craggy brook, for New York City's government was loathe to give up the tax revenue from a potential block of houses. Yet Ruggles convinced the city's aldermen that residences facing a park would generate higher taxes than if they faced additional houses on the proposed park land. His argument worked. On February 13, 1832, the City decreed: "… the lands composing such square shall be exempted from taxation and assessment." To this day, Gramercy Park remains the only private park in Manhattan. Ruggles' grandson dedicated a monument to him within the park, a lasting tribute to the pioneer who made this unique oasis possible.

It took over a decade to landscape the oasis; meanwhile, Ruggles sold the surrounding lots to some of America's most powerful men, who retained great architects to plan their new homes. James Renwick, famed for his design of Saint Patrick's Cathedral, designed the Calvary Church on the north side of the park. Calvert Vaux, co-designer of Central Park, built an opulent house at 15 Gramercy Park for Samuel Tilden, who lost the Presidential election in 1876 by one Electoral College vote. That carefully maintained manse is now the National Arts Club.

Other neighbors on or near the park soon included famed architect Stanford White, who redesigned many Gramercy Park interiors; Richard Morris Hunt, who later became known as the architect of the Metropolitan Museum; Cyrus Field, who laid the first transatlantic cable; inventor Peter Cooper, who earned a fortune on the B&O railroad and later built Cooper Union; authors Edith Wharton, Herman Melville, Stephen Crane, Nathanael West and O. Henry; composers Victor Herbert and Antonin Dvořák; and the nineteenth century's most acclaimed actor, Edwin Booth. Along with Mark Twain and Stanford White, Booth formed the Players Club, purchasing 16 Gramercy Park in 1888 for $75,000, which White remodeled into a clubhouse. It was Booth's home for the final five years of his life, and remains one of Gramercy Park's highlights.

A few years earlier, in 1857, Elisha Graves Otis had created a brilliant new gadget for hoisting heavy safes: he called his invention an elevator. His sons

^ Samuel B. Ruggles

expanded it to accommodate passengers, and installed three elevators in 34 Gramercy Park in 1883. With a tug on a rope within the elevator, water shifted between giant tanks in the basement and the rooftop, moving the elevator at fifty feet per minute as determined by the direction of the shifting water (a process still functioning within the building today, although the pump is no longer powered by steam). The result changed architecture, and Gramercy Park, forever.

The original building at 34 Gramercy had been a small hotel with stairs to each of its five stories. Demolished in 1880, new investors planned a taller hotel, with Louis Sherry's restaurant on the eighth floor. Before construction was completed, however, the investors opted not to proceed with the hotel, instead selling sixty five hundred shares in the building's corporation at $100 per share, allocated to units within the building. This historic action created the first cooperative apartment building in New York, an immediate sensation. Other co-ops soon followed; the concept of luxury apartment living soon displaced the charms of Gramercy Park's townhouses. More than half of them were demolished in the first half of the 20th century to make room for luxury flats.

Within thirty years, New York boasted an estimated forty thousand apartment houses. A new era had begun.

^ The view from 60 Gramercy Park North

14-1	First Co-op Building 34 Gramercy Park	**14-3**	Samuel Tilden House (National Arts Club) 15 Gramercy Park
14-2	Calvary Church 277 Park Avenue South	**14-4**	Players Club 16 Gramercy Park

Street Scenes in Old New York

Cab stand at Madison Square, 1900

Flatiron Building, 1902

Newsboys at Park Row, 1910

Clam seller in Mulberry Bend, ca. 1900

On the streets in a New York blizzard, 1899

Tending Stand, Canal Street, 1910

A load of kimonos just finished, Thompson Street, 1912

Miss Twombly, whip of Ladies Coach Run, and two other ladies beside coach on street, 1909

CHAPTER 15.

ASSASSINATION OF AN ARCHITECT

THE STORY OF STANFORD WHITE

The "trial of the century" and the scandalous demise of New York's foremost fin-de-siècle architect, Stanford White, is gleefully detailed in E.L. Doctorow's 1975 novel and the Broadway musical *Ragtime*. White's accomplishments while living merit a few songs too, for no Gilded Age designer succeeded better at charming New York's aristocrats, living in a style more ebullient than fiction, then leaving behind the architectural legacy that defines an era.

As the son of a journalist and theater reviewer, young Stanford took celebrity for granted at an early age. His father's friend Frederick Law Olmsted, the famed designer of Central Park, delivered sixteen-year-old Stanny to an architect, for whom he apprenticed shortly after the Civil War. The diversity of White's knowledge is astounding to modern professionals, for his grasp of clients' needs, command of exterior construction, and remarkable

‹ Stanford White's masterpiece, Madison Square Garden, 1901

application of interior details displays pure genius. He engineered building foundations that few would ever see, envisioned the exteriors that all might admire, then determined every decorative nuance, designing elements in stone, woodwork, glass, plaster, metals, and ceramics. Overseeing his project from concept to completion made Stanford White the darling of New York's gentry, as the city abounded with new construction. In 1879 he joined Charles McKim and William Rutherford Mead in forging the firm of McKim, Mead & White.

One of White's first projects was a splendid mansion on East 72nd Street for the famed jeweler Charles L. Tiffany, including a top floor apartment and massive studio for the jeweler's son Louis, who would soon gain fame as a decorative stained-glass artisan. From that day on, impressive commissions never ceased, including Judson Memorial Church at 55 Washington Square South, the Washington Square Arch, and his crowning achievement, the second Madison Square Garden at 26th Street and Madison Avenue.

Amid these impressive assignments, White lived beyond his means, collecting art, investing in shows, entertaining lavishly, often in the apartment he maintained atop Madison Square Garden. At age fifty, with his son studying architecture at Harvard while his wife occupied their elegant townhouse at 121 East 21st Street, Stanford began a scandalous affair with Evelyn Nesbit, a sixteen-year-old chorus girl appearing on Broadway in *Floradora*.

Two years later, Evelyn dumped him for actor John Barrymore, then married millionaire cocaine addict Harry K. Thaw, heir to a railroad fortune. Soon

after the marriage, upon learning that his wife's virginity had been lost years earlier to White, the enraged Thaw hired four private investigators to trail White.

On June 25, 1906, White attended the opening night of *Mamzelle Champagne,* a revue in which he invested.

^ Harry K. Thaw and Stanford White

In the middle of a number called "I Could Love a Million Girls," Thaw shot him three times at point blank range. White died instantly, and was buried on Long Island. Newspapers everywhere printed lurid details of the scandal for months.

^ Chorus girl Evelyn Nesbit at about age 16, 1900

Thaw was tried, declared not guilty by reason of insanity, and spent seven years in an asylum. Promptly upon his return to society, he divorced Evelyn. She returned to the stage, took drugs, attempted suicide, sold her story to the movies (she's played by youthful Joan Collins in *The Girl On The Red Velvet Swing*), and died in 1967 at age eighty two.

Despite his grand lifestyle, Stanford White died approximately $500,000 in debt. In four auctions, his treasures were sold. William Randolph Hearst bought his dining room ceiling for $3,000. The Metropolitan Museum acquired the baroque doorway from White's picture gallery. His wife retired to a modest Long Island cottage, and auctioned their remaining furniture during the Depression.

Stanford White's New York

Even better than the delightful songs in *Ragtime*, the happiest memories of Stanford White's prolific career can be celebrated throughout New York City. Though altered over time, his projects document an opulent Manhattan lifestyle that can no longer be replicated, including: the Villard Mansion on Madison Avenue at 50th Street (now the New York Palace), the Metropolitan Club (1 East 60th Street), the Harmonie Club (4 East 60th Street), the Players Club (16 Gramercy Park), the original Colony Club (120 Madison Avenue), 972 Fifth Avenue (now the French Embassy); the list goes on.

Among the "lost" buildings are: the second Madison Square Garden, the Herald Building (headquarters for the *New York Herald*), Sherry's Hotel (and its famous ice cream parlor at Fifth Avenue at 44th Street), and the glorious Penn Station (occupied by contemporary Madison Square Garden), which was completed after White's death.

^ **[top to bottom]**The Colony Club, Penn Station and the Villard Mansion

15-1	Tiffany Mansion East 72nd Street at Madison Avenue	**W-2**	Metropolitan Club: 1 East 60th Street
15-2	Judson Memorial Church 55 Washington Square South	**W-3**	Harmonie Club: 4 East 60th Street
15-3	Washington Square Arch Fifth Ave at Washington Square	**W-4**	Players Club: 16 Gramercy Park South
15-4	Madison Square Garden (1890) Madison Avenue at 26th Street	**W-5**	Colony Club (American Academy of Dramatic Arts): 120 Madison Avenue
15-5	White Townhouse: 121 East 21st Street	**W-6**	972 Fifth Avenue (French Embassy)
W-1	Villard Mansion Madison Avenue at 50th Street	**W-7**	Herald Building: Broadway at 34th Street
		W-8	Sherry's Hotel: Fifth Avenue at 44th St.
		W-9	The Original Penn Station: Eighth Avenue between 31st and 33rd streets

CHAPTER 16

ART IN AN ALLEY

THE ASHCAN SCHOOL AND THE CARRIAGE HOUSES OF GREENWICH VILLAGE

Stories abound about life in the magnificent brick town-houses along the northern edge of Washington Square, home to some of New York's most influential characters. The untold story is of the cobblestone alleys behind the elegant row, where socialites parked their horses and carriages.

In those days, New Yorkers traveled in horse-drawn carriages much the way we ride buses today, following specific routes and schedules. Only aristocrats could afford their own carriages and horses, along with the requisite housing that kept both safe from the elements. The carriage and the team, and sometimes even the stable boy, lived in a low-rise building near the family's townhouse. They weren't especially beautiful, but they were extremely practical, with high ceilings and wide doorframes through which to navigate the carriage, plus a loft or two above for hay and storage.

‹ Portrait of Dorothy Draper taken at New York University, 1840

Today, carriage houses remain scattered throughout the boroughs; the most notable ones are clustered in areas like Sniffen Court in Murray Hill, and in two beautiful cobblestone alleys in Greenwich Village: Washington Mews, accessible from Fifth Avenue and University Place, and MacDougal Alley, accessible from MacDougal Street just south of 8th Street.

Around the corner from the Washington Mews and those notable town-houses, John William Draper took his sister onto the roof of the Science Department at New York University in 1840. He snapped her picture with a primitive camera—this was the first image of a human face in sunlight. With the emergence of the camera, photographers like Jacob Riis and Matthew Brady, with his gut-wrenching photographs of Civil War battles, document-ed the realities of the moment.

As photographers began to chronicle the matter-of-fact, artists were left to dream and disturb convention in what they called "the new realism." Reject-ing the short, precise brush strokes of masters like Rembrandt, new artists defied reality and famously established Greenwich Village as America's primary art colony.

In 1858, Richard Morris Hunt designed the Tenth Street Studio Building, just east of Sixth Avenue, the country's first centralized facility for artists. It pro-vided light, privacy, and showrooms for its twenty-five residents, enabling painters and sculptors to live and work in single spacious studios, and thus, the "studio apartment" was born. The artists who embraced this radical lifestyle became some of the most revered names in American art: Winslow Homer, William Merritt Chase, and John LaFarge; their works hang in major museums today. An instant success, the Tenth Street Studios soon lured in-fluential critics, affluent patrons, and the curious public to its well-publicized "visiting days."

Other factors influenced the art scene. As New York's population exploded, the city's boundaries pushed northward, where snazzy buildings grew taller and taller. Greenwich Village, by contrast, looked dilapidated. The wealthy families of Washington Square had headed to fashionable surroundings uptown, relinquishing Greenwich Village to those who sought lower rents. Many townhouses were carved into tiny flats and rooming houses, and these became dense havens for writers, performers, musicians, and artists. Low-rise architecture guaranteed good sunlight for the artists and the rent was cheap. (As late as 1934, a four-room apartment on Grove Street was only $20 a month.)

Synergy among the bohemians was inevitable. As artists showcased their creations, Village writers trumpeted the news: Greenwich Village was the most inspired source of art in America. Across the street from the Tenth Street Studios, a collection of artists, including Stanford White and Augustus Saint-Gaudens, formed the Tile Club, reveling in the Village's creative energies.

Within adjacent blocks, the greatest American painters established their studios: John Singer Sargent, Grant Wood, George Bellows, Edward Hopper, the list continues impressively. And photography wasn't far behind. Matthew Brady opened a gallery nearby to display his Civil War photos. With no wealthy neighbors seeking shelter for their horses, the Village carriage houses were almost forgotten. Then came Gertrude Vanderbilt Whitney.

^ *The Tenth Street Studio* by William Merritt Chase, 1880

In 1907, the enormously wealthy Whitney planned a career as a sculptor, which required a workspace with a high ceiling. She struck up friendships with local artists, and rented 19 MacDougal Alley.

The carriage house made a perfect studio: sunlight streamed through its high, wide doorframe, while the ceiling height guaranteed the creative space every sculptor needs. Mrs. Whitney soon became a patron to several artists working in or near the carriage houses; in 1914, their first group show in the remodeled MacDougal Alley studio caused an uproar.

Critics and patrons accustomed to plush surroundings sneered at art displayed in an alley, especially since it audaciously depicted the grimier details of life. The artists were dubbed the Ashcan School, a distinction they wore with pride. Artist Robert Henri was an admirer of the down-to-earth realism of artists like Thomas Eakins; other Ashcan artists included George Bellows, William Glackens, George Luks, Everett Shinn, and John Sloan. Mrs. Whitney bought four of their paintings and a building at 8 West 8th Street to display them. The Whitney Museum of American Art was born.

For the first half of the twentieth century, some of the greatest names in modern art—Mark Rothko, Barnett Newman, Jackson Pollock, and Robert Motherwell—thrived on the bohemian energy of Greenwich Village. The Ashcan artists eventually moved on to greater fame and larger spaces, while the carriage houses were transformed into homes. Their great doorframes were sealed to become picture windows, plumbing and heat were installed, and soon the former stables were small but valuable homes in quaint Village cul-de-sacs. Today, the Washington Mews carriage houses are part of New York University and the Whitney Museum lives uptown.

^ Gertrude Vanderbilt Whitney poses for the January 1917 issue of *Vogue* magazine

16-1 Sniffen Court

16-2 Washington Mews

16-3 MacDougal Alley

16-4 Tenth Street Studio
51 West 10th Street

16-5 Tile Club
58 West 10th Street

16-6 Gertrude Whitney's Gallery
8 West 8th Street

CHAPTER 17.

APARTMENT LIFE

THE DAKOTA AND THE GOLDEN AGE

Once upon a time in New York, anyone who was anyone resided in a townhouse, while aspiring to own a Fifth Avenue mansion. Yet, with the advent of apartment living at The Dakota in 1884, New Yorkers abandoned their brownstone stoops to head for the elevators.

Townhouses offered cross-ventilation, ample rooms for children and storage, special entrances for servants, backyards for beating the carpets. Why would anyone forego these urban conveniences to live anonymously, stacked beneath other similarly-miserable denizens? Undesirable, multiple-unit buildings flourished in many squalid pockets across the city. Those noisy, drafty, and unsafe tenements housed the immigrant peasants who arrived in staggering multitudes daily at Ellis Island to work in sweatshops. Every resident in a tenement flat dreamed of escaping such squalor. Who would choose to live like them?

But New Yorkers knew other facts about those apartment flats. Unlike the best townhouses on Washington Square, tenements had real indoor plumb-

‹ Ice skaters enjoy Central Park with The Dakota in the background, 1894 ing; no outhouses, no cisterns, no chamber pots. It was not uncommon for a servant to labor all day in a high-profile townhouse, only to return to more modern amenities in an apartment. Soon, Edward Clark, co-owner of the Singer Sewing Machine Company, recognized several oncoming trends and devised a radical scheme.

Clark saw that New York was a boomtown. Business was great, thanks to the steady supply of cheap European labor. And, thanks to the Industrial Revolution, businesses were expanding exponentially; as more companies opened, more employees were flocking to New York. Housing just couldn't keep pace with demand, one reason why tenements were so grossly overpopulated. Yet Clark knew that in European cities, the gentry had been living in elegant flats for decades. Surmising that the resistance to apartment life in America stemmed solely from the negative associations New Yorkers made as they observed the discomforts of tenement dwellers, Clark seized the opportunity to erect a building that could never be confused with a tenement.

Dubbed "Clark's Folly" while it was being constructed, The Dakota earned its name by being located so far beyond metropolitan New York that visitors exclaimed that they were traveling to Dakota Territory. Clark knew his building's success would stem from his marketing acumen. By word of mouth alone, he sold the amenities as strongly as the apartments themselves. The Dakota offered two top floors of servants' rooms for the staff of the primary residents below, while the second floor was designed as a collection of hotel-style suites for tenants to house their visiting guests. Since a carriage ride in 1884 from Washington Square to The Dakota required half a day, dark approached by the time a guest completed a social call at The Dakota. Fearing nighttime assaults by Eighth Avenue "highwaymen", an overnight stay in The Dakota became a welcomed ritual. After all, it was the only apartment house in America with four passenger elevators. It also boasted over two hundred miles of plumbing.

The overnight guestrooms were a stroke of marketing genius. As visitors became more comfortable with the Dakota's location and the new Central Park, the viability of an entire neighborhood was born. Still unfinished when the building first opened, Clark installed a mini-Con Edison underground in the adjacent lot, with furnaces massive enough to provide steam not just to The Dakota, but to "all the blocks from the north side of 70th Street to the south

side of 74th Street between Eighth and Columbus Avenues" along with generators for "electric
illumination." (There was no electricity above
Spruce Street in 1884.) For those traditionalists
who preferred fireplaces—Clark's apartment had
seventeen—the building's staff provided fire-
wood and coal, and ashes were swept out daily.

Unlike the low ceilings of most townhouses
(where high ceilings just meant more stairs to
climb), life in a "French flat," as architect Henry
Hardenbergh put it, provided rooms on a grand
scale. Apartments on low floors at The Dakota had fifteen-foot ceilings, while
servants' quarters featured twelve-foot ceiling heights, and just about every
apartment had a drawing room, some the size of ballrooms.

Upon the building's completion on October 27, 1884, the *New York Graphic*
published a twenty-five hundred-word article that called The Dakota "the
most perfect apartment house in the world." The story gushed that The
Dakota "guaranteed to the tenants comforts which would require unlimited
wealth in a private residence." It was the endorsement Clark longed to hear,
for it confirmed the viability of luxury apartments, the first in the Western
Hemisphere. But sadly, unbeknownst to many tenants, Clark died almost
two years before the building's completion. He left the entire ownership of
The Dakota to his grandson who was also his namesake. When the building
opened and the money flooded in, tenants wrote their monthly rent checks
to their landlord Edward S. Clark, a twelve-year-old boy.

Following the *New York Graphic* story, which was reprinted in the *New York
Times*, downtowners thronged to the city's newest attraction with hundreds
of requests for apartments, but it was too late. Without a single advertisement, The Dakota was fully rented; a ten-room apartment went for $3,000
per year. Townhouses were abruptly passé; the Age of the Apartment House
had arrived. Once again, construction could not keep pace with demand.

Now architects and builders faced a new problem. How quickly could they
meet the demands of consumers who suddenly wished to live in luxury
flats? Who even knew how to design or build one of those newfangled

^ Edward Clark

"skyscrapers?" Into this uncertain environment came Emery Roth, one of the most prolific but uncelebrated architects in New York history. With luck, good timing, and spectacular craftsmanship, Emery Roth permanently changed the New York City skyline, designing the most magnificent residences the city had ever seen.

Emery Roth was a Hungarian-Jewish immigrant with no formal training. He apprenticed to the architects that built the World's Columbian Exposition in Chicago in 1893, then came to New York, where Richard Morris Hunt's firm paid him $25 per week to sketch private residences. He also studied the Stuyvesant Apartments built by Hunt on East 18th Street, where "luxury flats" accessed by elevators had private indoor plumbing, unlike the squalid tenements nearby.

In 1899, Roth secured his first major commission: the Saxony Apartments on Broadway and 82nd Street, followed soon after by the Hotel Belleclaire on Broadway at 77th Street, the first residential structure in Manhattan to be entirely supported by a steel frame.

As the Hotel Belleclaire was rising above Broadway, Leo and Alexander Bing arrived at Roth's office; they were brothers who sold plots of land to speculative builders, then provided the building loans. Observing his knowledge of modern high-rise architecture, the brothers proposed that Roth oversee their upcoming projects, a relationship that stretched over three decades, as Roth designed forty-five buildings for Bing & Bing, from Greenwich Village to Washington Heights.

Meanwhile, New York was in turmoil. Between 1899 and 1913, the assessed value of Manhattan real estate increased by two hundred and seven percent. Well-to-do families, seeking refuge from Manhattan's rapidly escalating taxes, felt forced to abandon their single-family homes. However, popular sentiment observed that apartments were now homes for millionaires, too, perhaps with more rooms than a brownstone, all on one floor, plus multiple baths and servants' quarters.

When the trains in the tunnel under Park Avenue were electrified in 1905, the noise and soot subsided. Park Avenue became the grand new boulevard where Roth could develop large plots of land into high-rise apartment houses. His first Park Avenue construction was the graceful 570 Park, built of white marble and red brick, decorated with white terra cotta. He designed the facade of 417 Park, constructed entirely of limestone. At 1000 Park Avenue, he designed a massive building of brown brick. The two gothic figures that flank the main entrance, one a warrior and the other a builder, are rumored to be modeled after his clients Leo and Alexander Bing.

Following World War I, America's consumer purchasing power increased dramatically. The pent-up demand for housing stimulated an enormous construction boom, especially in New York. From 1920 to 1930, New York City accounted for twenty percent of all residential construction in the entire nation. Back in 1919, apartment buildings accounted for only about thirty-nine percent of new construction; by 1926, that figure was seventy-seven percent. With hotels included, high-rise residential buildings accounted for eighty-five percent of all construction in New York City between 1927 and 1930. Townhouses were history.

This was an era of great prosperity, and the golden age of apartment house construction; Emery Roth's skills were in high demand all over town. He designed majestic focal points such as 480 Park Avenue, along with less prominent "background buildings" including 221 West 82nd Street and 228 West 83rd Street. For Bing & Bing he created 39 Fifth Avenue, 10 Sheridan Square, and 310 West End Avenue. Controversy arose when Bing & Bing constructed Roth's design for the Hotel Dorset at 30 West 54th Street, a large building on the same narrow block as the hallowed mansion of John D. Rockefeller, Jr. To escape the invasion of businesses and apartment houses, the Rockefellers moved away.

Roth continued to develop hotels, designing the Drake at 440 Park Avenue and the Alden at 222 Central Park West, his eventual home after his children had grown. Along Fifth Avenue, he designed 1115, 1125, 1133, and 1200, as well as 784, 1009, 1112, and 1175 Park Avenue.

To encourage new construction, New York City redefined its zoning laws, permitting high-rises where modest five-story dwellings once stood. The new zoning laws were put to the test when Emery Roth was retained to create the Ritz Tower at Park Avenue and 57th Street in 1926. Unlike the fifteen-story buildings he frequently called his "skyscratchers," the Ritz reached a soaring forty-one stories, dominating the Manhattan skyline, a true residential skyscraper. From the top of the completed building, an unbroken view opened for twenty-five miles in every direction, which Roth proclaimed to be "a panorama unexcelled in all New York." Although at least one critic referred to it as a "skypuncture," New Yorkers understood the need for this new generation of slender, stepped-back towers of unprecedented heights.

Roth planned opulence in every corner of the Ritz Tower, from grand entertaining rooms on the ground floor, profuse ornamentation inside and out, to a new kind of cooperative arrangement for maids and valets. Instead of providing servants' quarters within individual units, the Ritz Tower provided a staff for all tenants. Servants wages were included in the rent, an appealing amenity to wealthy tenants seeking to reduce their daily expenses without compromising their lifestyles. At the opening banquet on November 15, 1926, Mayor Jimmy Walker and other distinguished New Yorkers unanimously praised the labors of Emery Roth, the self-taught immigrant whose work represented the cutting edge of ingenuity.

Roth was soon awarded his two most important commissions: the Beresford and the San Remo on Central Park West. Situated at a corner where two parks—Central Park and Manhattan Square, home to the American Museum of Natural History—meet, the Beresford rises twenty-two stories and from a distance resembles an impregnable fortress; upon closer inspection it blends harmoniously into its site.

Similar luxury was built into the San Remo to far more startling effect. Studying the new zoning laws, Roth understood that residential buildings could achieve new heights if setbacks and courtyards were provided in exchange. He devised the first twin-towered skyscraper, adding two eleven-story towers above the San Remo's seventeen-story base. The ingenious concept completely eliminated the need for hallways, since each tower floor was occupied by one private apartment, with light and air from every direction, along with views as glorious as those at the Ritz.

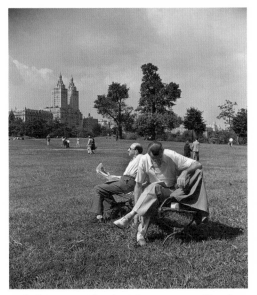

Then the bubble burst. As the stock market crashed in 1929, the San Remo failed to lure wealthy tenants. One year after its construction, thirty percent of the apartments remained vacant. In Central Park, directly across from the San Remo's sparkling lobby, penniless people built shanties of tin and tarpaper. The bank that held the San Remo's mortgage collapsed just months after the building opened; its officers were indicted for speculating with depositors' funds. After a series of bankruptcies and rent rollbacks, the largest apartments were subdivided. Every two-story apartment in the south tower was cut into two single-floor units. The Beresford suffered a similar fate. In 1940, the San Remo and the Beresford were sold together for $25,000 cash over the existing mortgages. In 1929, the buildings had been valued at approximately $10 million. The golden age of apartment construction was over. No one, not even Emery Roth erected buildings like those ever again.

Just as America entered World War II, Roth was commissioned to build 875 Fifth Avenue, (possibly the last building any broker can call "prewar"). To erect the building, three grand mansions were to be razed, including one designed by Roth's mentor, Richard M. Hunt. When the war ended, Emery was retained to build a cooperative at 880 Fifth Avenue, across the street from his recent project. Displaying the plans to his son Richard, who had just returned home from the Navy, the younger Roth's suggestions for revisions were so extensive that Emery recognized that this was the project to pass to his son. At the corner of Fifth Avenue and 69th Street, Emery's final building, 875 Fifth Avenue, stands on the foundation of his mentor, facing the first project developed by his son: 880 Fifth Avenue. The firm of Emery Roth and Sons was established months later.

^ Central Park with the San Remo in the background, 1942

New York Residences by Emery Roth and Sons

San Remo

10 Sheridan Square

Ritz Tower

417 Park Avenue

The Beresford

480 Park Avenue

39 Fifth Avenue

880 Fifth Avenue

875 Fifth Avenue

17-1	The Dakota
17-2	Saxony Apartments
17-3	Hotel Belleclaire
17-4	570 Park Avenue
17-5	417 Park Avenue
17-6	1000 Park Avenue
17-7	480 Park Avenue
17-8	221 West 82nd Street
17-9	228 West 83rd Street
17-10	39 Fifth Avenue

17-11	10 Sheridan Square
17-12	310 West End Avenue
17-13	Hotel Dorset
17-14	The Drake
17-15	The Alden
17-16	1115 Fifth Avenue
17-17	1125 Fifth Avenue
17-18	1133 Fifth Avenue
17-19	1200 Fifth Avenue
17-20	784 Park Avenue

17-21	1009 Park Avenue
17-22	1112 Park Avenue
17-23	1175 Park Avenue
17-24	Ritz Tower
17-25	The Beresford
17-26	San Remo
17-27	875 Fifth Avenue
17-28	880 Fifth Avenue

CHAPTER 18.

LOWER EAST SIDE

AN IMMIGRANT TALE

In 1900, it was tough to be a Jew in Europe. Russian pogroms pushed people from their homes, dividing families through needless violence and intolerance. Other nations forced other indignities, leading many Jews to give up their homes in Europe to pursue new lives elsewhere. For many, Ellis Island in New York Harbor was the first stop.

Great waves of Jewish immigrants arrived in Manhattan during the first decades of the twentieth century. Although they came from Russia, Prussia, Austria-Hungary, Lithuania and many other nations, these immigrants found unity through the Yiddish language they all shared. They settled into the tenements to the east of Little Italy in the Lower East Side, a neighborhood that stretches from Canal Street up to Houston Street, from the Bowery to the East River.

By 1915, three hundred and twenty thousand Jews lived on the Lower East Side, making it one of the most densely populated places in America. Most tenements were constructed with four apartments per floor, with bathtubs

‹ Orchard Street on a Sunday morning, 1916

in the kitchens and communal toilets out in the hall. In the humid New York summer, the fire escape provided a place to sleep, away from the tenement's stale air. The neighborhood became known for its ethnic cuisine, places like Guss' Pickles, Katz's Deli, Yonah Shimmel's Knishery became local institutions that serve traditional food to this day.

Not everyone was Jewish. Italians, Poles and other Eastern-Europeans joined in the mix, united in their poverty as well as in their aspirations for a bright new start in America. In the early twentieth century, jobs were controlled by ethnicities in matter-of-fact New York. Irishmen were cops, the Chinese ran the laundries, Germans owned the breweries; soon the residents of the Lower East Side became famous for developing New York's garment industry

THE LOWER EAST SIDE TODAY
Discover the Lower East Side's rich history at the Lower East Side Tenement Museum, which offers guided tours of a restored nineteenth-century tenement at 97 Orchard Street.

Then, taste the neighborhood's history at nearby shop The Pickle Guys, 49 Essex Street, between Grand and Hester streets.

^ The Cottone family works together finishing garments in an Extra Place tenement, hoping to make $2 a week, 1913 into a national powerhouse. The sweatshops along Broadway were packed with laborers from the Lower East Side: pieceworkers who were paid by the number of sleeves or zippers or pockets they sewed. Tailors who owned their own sewing machines frequently strapped those machines to their backs, then took extra work home each night. The garment industry moved uptown (and around the world).

In the past twenty years, the neighborhood has undergone one of the most remarkable transformations the city has ever seen. Once a symbol of urban blight, today the Lower East Side is now gentrified almost beyond recognition. The artists arrived first, followed by luxury developers during the boom years of the early twenty-first century. Now, luxurious apartments stand beside tenements, trendy cafés and hip nightspots, even a brand-new Whole Foods and the shimmering New Museum of Contemporary Art occupy prominent locations in the ever evolving, ever exciting neighborhood.

18-1 Pickle Guys 49 Essex Street		**18-4** New Museum 235 Bowery	
18-2 Katz' Deli 205 East Houston		**18-5** Lower East Side Tenement Museum: 97 Orchard St.	
18-3 Yonah Shimmel's Knishery 137 East Houston Street			

CHAPTER 19

PROHIBITION AND ALL THAT JAZZ

THE SPEAKEASY DAYS OF NEW YORK CITY

Good times abounded in 1918 when World War I ended. New Yorkers embraced bold new lifestyles; wealthy families gave up their costly mansions for modern apartments in Park Avenue "skyscrapers." Gone were formal dinners of grand cuisine: "cocktail parties" were all the rage. Women gained the right to vote, then promptly cut their hair and hemlines, exposing calves for the first time in a millennium. Couples who once waltzed at arms length now tangoed cheek-to-cheek, while "flappers" danced the Charleston to the newfangled rhythm called jazz.

It was too good to remain unchallenged. When a Minnesota Congressman introduced an Amendment to the U.S. Constitution that made alcoholic beverages illegal, America faced a political cataclysm. In a puritanical tantrum,

‹ Police Commissioner John Leach watches as agents pour liquor into the sewer after a raid during the height of Prohibition, 1921 the House and Senate overrode President Wilson's veto, making Prohibition a federal law on January 16, 1920. The nation's new wave of morality crashed hard against New York's good time revolution. Manhattan real estate was soon put to some surprising new uses.

"No liquor?!" The federal government padlocked about sixteen thousand barrooms in New York, while the highest-profile restaurants in New York closed rather than serve meals without champagne or cocktails. Famous institutions like Delmonico's were shuttered, while Louis Sherry turned his celebrated cafe into an ice cream parlor. One French restaurant clung to business by mixing water or seltzer into its wines, reducing the alcohol level to an acceptable three percent, but New Yorkers weren't buying it. Instead, they supported a far more clandestine industry: illegal "speakeasies" where hard liquor came with assorted adventures. New York soon had an estimated thirty-two thousand speakeasies as Prohibition ratcheted up the excitement of living in the Jazz age.

The first place for speakeasies to proliferate was, predictably, in Greenwich Village. New York's bohemia was the ideal spot for celebrating the civil liberties society attempted to deny, and drinking became an act of defying authority. Through the Village's maze of winding side streets, walk-up apartments turned into distribution centers for homemade spirits. Village "tea rooms," once renowned as gathering places for intellectuals, evolved into cabarets, providing entertainment and mediocre food along with a steady supply of homemade red wine, thanks to the area's large Italian population.

The illegal beverage consumption was hidden behind closed doors and shuttered windows. Patrons were scrutinized from behind front door peepholes, admitted by tough guys who were always on the alert for raids by the vice squads. With money ready, these guys paid off the police. The demand for quality liquor gave rise to "bootleggers," the dispensers of illegal American-made spirits, and to smuggling, as gangsters imported spirits from Canada and abroad for distribution in the U.S.

Speakeasy owners found themselves millionaires practically overnight, with business obligations that could best be handled by professional strong-arm men. The result was termed organized crime, as these gangsters provided protection for their clubs, sharing part of the profits with local politicians to keep the vice squads away. Meanwhile, New York's vice squad was laughingly known as the training class for the best new bootleggers, as federal agents gave up their civil servant salaries in exchange for fortunes reaped by joining the other side of the law. The work was just as dangerous, but the pay was better. Besides, a vice agent-turned-bootlegger already had contacts with politicians, knew all the competitors, and knew what actions might be coming next from the federal government.

Thanks to liquor, Greenwich Village was suddenly a destination; its cabarets filled not just by its local residents, but by anyone seeking excitement, which Village clubs notoriously provided. It was a sexual meeting ground, where fantasy clubs were decorated like pirate's dens, prison cells, and country barns. It was a place where gay people could congregate in relative comfort.

Entrepreneurs soon realized that clandestine operations could generate more income with other forms of "entertainment." A blacksmith's shop with its primary entrance in Pamela Court at 58 Barrow Street became Chumley's, with a secret, unmarked door around the corner (86 Bedford Street) for patrons to escape if (and when) the bar was raided for selling illegal spirits.

However, the secret speakeasy was actually a cover for the even more furtive casino upstairs. A dumbwaiter large enough to transport two adults at a time led from Chumley's kitchen to the second floor of 58 Barrow Street, where gamblers placed their bets into the wee hours.

^ Tap dancer Bill "Bojangles" Robinson, 1933

Old real estate was put to new use, generating even greater profit. During Prohibition, Mayor Jimmy Walker, a celebrated reveler himself, debated with the Board of Estimate about removing the residential zoning from either 52nd or 55th Street to accommodate the dining needs of theatergoers. After contemplation, they stripped the residential zoning from both streets. The once-elegant brownstones soon housed scores of speakeasies on lower floors, while upper levels were divided into flats populated by kept women, gigolos, more than one brothel, and the alleged residence of mobster "Legs" Diamond.

The 21 Club (at 21 West 52nd Street, then called Jack and Charlie's) hid over five thousand cases of booze behind a trick basement wall where it remained undetected by authorities. Fifty-second Street soon became known simply as "The Street." Jazz musicians hopped from one speakeasy to another, while celebrities such as Jimmy Durante, George Murphy, and Ruby Keeler performed in smoky bars. The value of real estate in the West 50s skyrocketed.

Meanwhile, black Harlem became a congested place bursting with street life. As parties simmered down in the speakeasies of the West 50s, Harlem clubs were picking up steam. Large cabarets like the Savoy Ballroom and the Cotton Club featured dazzling entertainers that defined the Jazz age, from Duke Ellington's band to magnificent vocalists like Bessie Smith, Ethel Waters, and Bill "Bojangles" Robinson. The proprietors, most of them white, paid plenty to keep from being raided for serving bootleg booze, a cost they passed on to their predominantly white patrons, who were only too ready to pay for memorable evenings in Harlem's netherworld.

Prohibition officially ended in 1932 when the federal government repealed its misguided amendment, but one final wallop redefined New York's political system. To celebrate Prohibition's repeal, Mayor Jimmy Walker led a "Beer Parade" down Fifth Avenue, his last public appearance before facing charges brought by New York Governor Franklin Roosevelt. In previous months, a succession of Walker administration officials had difficulty explaining how their modest salaries generated personal fortunes, upon which taxes were often unpaid. Even Thomas Farley, the sheriff of New York County, couldn't explain how he amassed nearly a half-million dollars in six years on an annual salary of $8,500.

In courtroom testimony, it became apparent that not only were city officials accepting graft while permitting the sale and consumption of alcohol, but in the process, they accepted payoffs for just about everything else. Add an extra floor to a skyscraper without a variance? Just slip $3,000 to the Buildings Inspector. Dock a transatlantic ocean liner on a Hudson River pier? Pay $50,000 in unmarked bills. After months of courtroom wrangling and media scandal, Mayor Walker resigned from office, Governor Roosevelt ran for President, and the new mayor, Fiorello La Guardia, cleaned up much of the corruption within New York City's government.

Now legal, most speakeasies simply removed the peepholes from their front doors and openly welcomed the paying public. With easy access to legal liquor, white patrons were less inclined to visit Harlem, where clubs faded away, street congestion diminished, and rents were reduced as supply exceeded demand. The effects of Prohibition were felt for decades, but fortunately, today in New York, it's not that exciting to buy a friend a drink.

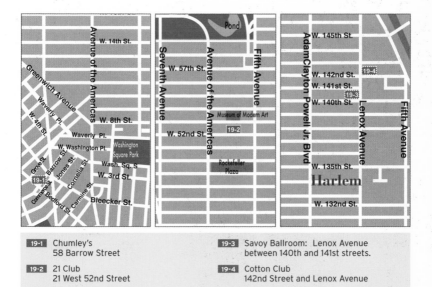

19-1 Chumley's
58 Barrow Street

19-2 21 Club
21 West 52nd Street

19-3 Savoy Ballroom: Lenox Avenue
between 140th and 141st streets.

19-4 Cotton Club
142nd Street and Lenox Avenue

CHAPTER 20

A HARLEM HISTORY

PHILIP A. PAYTON
BUILDS A NEIGHBORHOOD

There is probably no real estate broker anywhere in twentieth-century America who has done more to develop a neighborhood, advance a cause, and launch a culture than Philip A. Payton Jr. The neighborhood was Harlem at the turn of the twentieth century; Payton was the visionary who encouraged its development into America's preeminent black community. But let's start at the beginning.

Harlem wasn't always a black enclave. Originally settled in 1658 by Peter Stuyvesant under Dutch rule, Nieuw Haarlem was lush agricultural land distinctly separate from Nieuw Amsterdam at Manhattan's southern tip. For generations, the sole connection between the settlements was a diagonal road built on an old Indian path: today's Broadway. Following the War of 1812, agriculture gave way to commerce as farms were divided into Manhattan's now-familiar grid of streets and avenues, connecting rural Harlem, at least on paper, to the busy city to its south.

‹ A crowd outside Harlem's Savoy Ballroom, 1952

With the opening of the Harlem Railroad in the 1830s, and the Second and Third Avenue Railroads in 1879 and 1880, hundreds of tenement apartments were erected east of Third Avenue and north of 100th Street. Removed from the primary business hub downtown, Harlem residents made a compromise: spend nearly two hours each day on the trains, in an era when people routinely worked twelve hours per day, six days a week, in exchange for lower rents and an escape from the overcrowded tenements downtown. While the fare from the Battery to Harlem was fifteen cents each way, a special "rush hour" fare of seven cents was offered to commuters between 5:30 and seven a.m. and again in the evening from five to seven. It worked. Apartment houses built on speculation were soon filled with new residents. The once-sparse landscape blossomed into a desirable new "suburb" of Jewish, Italian, German, and Irish immigrants. When vaudeville impresario Oscar Hammerstein built the Harlem Opera House on 125th Street in 1889, Harlem became a destination.

As word got out in 1902 that the Interborough Rapid Transit would open subway stations along Harlem's west side, speculative builders wasted no time. Avoiding the low-rent tenements of Harlem's east side, many builders opted for grander and costlier dwellings: luxury apartment houses with elevators; spacious townhouses with marble mantels and parquet floors. Soon after the grand subway opening of 1904, those builders were clobbered by harsh reality: in their zeal to develop Harlem's west side, they had overestimated the market. The supply of residential real estate was far greater than its demand. New apartments and townhouses stood half-empty while real estate taxes and mortgage repayments squeezed speculator's cash flow. Harlem was a real estate bust.

Meanwhile, a small black population settled in the area near Greeley Square at 34th Street and Broadway. With the arrival of Macy's and Gimbel's department stores, residential buildings were being demolished to accommodate the new shopping district. The black residents were forced to move: never an easy prospect, since landlords throughout New York could legally refuse to rent to people of color. Enter Philip Payton, a black man succeeding as a professional real estate broker in an era when African-Americans regularly faced discrimination in employment. Learning of the black families' plights and observing the empty properties in Harlem, Payton made the deal that changed Manhattan. He convinced financially strapped landlords to accept "colored" residents. He then led low-income black families to spacious new homes in Harlem, places they could not afford, and convinced them to double up, or sublet an extra room or two to make ends meet.

Landlords begrudgingly viewed Payton's plan as the only solution to their cash-flow crunch, especially when Payton extracted higher rents from his black tenants than landlords would get from whites. Tenants, too, had to get used to the idea of an extra boarder in their midst, but faced with limited choices in housing, Payton's economic balance worked. In the process, the black residents of Harlem developed a close-knit community. Within a decade, Harlem became one of the most densely populated areas in the entire nation.

In 1920, there were about one hundred and fifty thousand African-Americans living in New York and a hundred thousand of them lived in Harlem. By 1929, New York's black population had exploded to three hundred and twenty-seven thousand. Payton prospered, buying property on 134th Street at Fifth Avenue that he developed into housing for more black neighbors. Other landlords resisted. The Kortwright Apartments at 1990 Seventh Avenue, for example, didn't admit black tenants until 1926.

Rather than rent to dwindling numbers of white tenants, some landlords listed their buildings for sale; enterprising blacks pooled their resources and bought the buildings themselves. By 1925, African-Americans owned an estimated $60 million worth of Harlem real estate. Although the population boomed, the boundaries of the two-mile-long neighborhood barely expanded. As black neighborhoods became more densely populated, lines of segregation hardened.

In the years between the two World Wars, Harlem was filled with promise. Calling it "Dreamland" and "Black Mecca," entertainers touring America spoke with pride of the burgeoning community in Harlem. With soil exhaustion and the boll weevil pushing Southern blacks away from the land, Harlem became a destination of almost mythical proportions, where

^ Philip A. Payton

manufacturing jobs, a united community, and an escape from poll taxes and Jim Crow laws awaited. It was exotic, colorful, sensuous; a place that partied late into the night. The Cotton Club, Harlem's most exclusive nightspot, presented black headliners like Duke Ellington, Pearl Bailey and Lena Horne to a whites-only audience that was grateful for the bootleg liquor that accompanied its stellar entertainment.

However, for a mere 40 cents at the door, dancers of all colors could swing all night in the Savoy Ballroom, to the sounds of jazz improvisers like Louis Armstrong, Earl Hines, and Coleman Hawkins. Elsewhere, tenants threw rent parties, paying anywhere from a dime to a half-dollar to cover a hard-luck-host's rent before the furniture landed on the sidewalk on the first of the month. Three-piece "pick-up bands," wailed their jazz through those dimly lit apartments, while amateur singers belted out popular radio songs. Some of the most gifted unemployed musicians of the 1930s played in Harlem's hallways, apartments and yards.

Harlem's success sparkled on brownstone streets like Strivers' Row (West 138th to 139th Streets, between Adam Clayton Powell Jr. Boulevard and Frederick Douglass Boulevard), home to jazz pianist Eubie Blake, songwriter Noble Sissle, and W. C. Handy, the "Father of the Blues."

What ended the good times? In the Depression years, overcrowding and poverty were stifling. When Prohibition ended in 1933, Harlem's nightlife instantly declined. Clubs moved closer to their wealthier white patrons downtown; the music industry moved to Hollywood, and most jazz greats followed. Only a few clubs remained, like the Apollo Theater on 125th Street, now a testament to Harlem's durability.

Drug-related crimes drove away much of the population. By the 1970s, Harlem was again a real estate bust, with half-empty buildings wedged between prison-like housing projects.

But by the end of the twentieth century, Harlem reclaimed its status as a haven for real-estate buyers, families and young professionals. New shops and exciting clubs invited another generation to celebrate uptown, while investors of all colors restore Harlem's brownstones and its legacy. Be prepared, kids: The cost of train fare is no longer 15 cents.

- **20-1** Harlem Opera House: 207 West 125th Street
- **20-2** Greeley Square: 34th Street and Broadway
- **20-3** Philip Payton's Purchase: 134th Street at Fifth Avenue
- **20-4** Kortwright Apartments: 1990 Seventh Avenue
- **20-5** Cotton Club: 142nd Street and Lenox Avenue
- **20-6** Savoy Ballroom
  Lenox Avenue between 140th and 141st streets
- **20-7** Strivers' Row: West 138th and 139th streets
- **20-8** Apollo Theater: 253 West 125th Street

CHAPTER 21

THE MASTER BUILDER

THE CONTROVERSIAL CHARACTER OF ROBERT MOSES

Imagine a highway running straight across Soho, and the Village without Washington Square. Unthinkable.

These plans and many like them were real designs for Manhattan not so long ago. As New York's urban environment evolves to accommodate the demands of the lives and industries within it, urban planners sometimes conceived of wild notions in their efforts to fashion the best future for the city. For most of the twentieth century, a single mastermind dominated notions of urban design: Parks Commissioner Robert Moses. Admired and reviled, no strategist ever held more power or reshaped an American city as boldly. Moses' is an angry story of dreams, schemes, and tax dollars at work.

There is hardly a vista in any of New York's five boroughs that does not include Robert Moses' imprint. He built public works on a scale unmatched by any other individual in American history. By ramming bulkheads of steel beneath rivers and harbors, then covering them with stone and cement, his teams created fifteen thousand acres of new land, permanently altering the physical boundaries of the city.

‹ The Triborough Bridge, 1937

In Lower Manhattan, he approved public housing for five hundred fifty-five thousand tenants (that's larger than the population of Wyoming), then built another giant complex, Co-op City, in the Bronx. He gave the city six hundred fifty-eight playgrounds, six hundred seventy-three baseball diamonds, and two hundred eighty-eight tennis courts; his convoys of trucks hauled the city's garbage into marshes that were then covered with earth and lawn to become more parks. From the Triborough Bridge (which was recently renamed after Robert F. Kennedy) to the Verrazano, plus Madison Square Garden, Lincoln Center, Shea Stadium and Jones Beach, Robert Moses brought his dreams to fruition. In the process, he evicted hundreds of thousands of New Yorkers from their homes, tore down buildings and constructed new ones according to his vision. Entire neighborhoods were obliterated at his command. Lives changed at his whim.

As a young attorney in 1924, Robert Moses met Governor Alfred E. Smith, who liked Moses' enthusiasm when discussing a new concept: a state park. Twenty-nine states didn't have any; six had one each. At the governor's suggestion, Moses drafted a bill establishing the Long Island State Park Commission, installing himself as president, then tackled his new assignment with vigor. With an increasing number of New Yorkers learning to drive, Moses noted that New York's streets were designed for horses and carriages. No major American city had expressways to accommodate rapid transit. If New Yorkers were ever to visit a state park on Long Island, there would have to be a State Parkway first. After months of tramping across sand spits and Long Island woodlands, Robert Moses mapped out a system of state parks covering forty thousand acres, linked by broad parkways to New York City. He was soon embroiled in years of scrappy vendettas against wealthy Long Island property owners, while acquiring land for the parkways through eminent domain, the legal concept that empowers the government to acquire privately owned land for public use. Those battles were forgiven when the magnificent Jones Beach State Park opened in 1929.

The press and public hailed Moses' vision; architects from Europe praised Jones Beach as "the finest seashore playground ever given the public anywhere in the world." More importantly, businesses clamored for locations near those parkway exits, spawning new construction, more jobs, and yes, new tax revenues for towns across Long Island. Politicians and schoolchildren alike cheered for Mr. Moses.

In 1933, Mayor La Guardia invited Robert Moses to work his magic in New York City. Moses' reply: he would become the city's first Parks Commissioner only if he could also control its parkways and keep his state job.

With the governor and every local politician watching, the mayor consented. Moses then drafted the Triborough Act, an authority so cunning that it's still studied in colleges today. Its passage empowered his Triborough Authority to issue forty-year bonds to underwrite new bridges, parks, and roadways, with one clever catch: the existence of the Triborough Authority "shall continue only until its bonds have been paid in full." However, "The authority shall have power to refund any bonds by the issuance of new bonds, whether the bonds to be refunded have or have not matured, [to be used] for any other corporate purpose."

In other words, bonds would never mature, because the Authority would simply reissue those bonds, which were technically "new" for another forty years. As long as there were bonds outstanding, the Triborough Authority remained in business, and so did Commissioner Moses. Further, as president of the Authority, Moses was completely autonomous; no City Council could shut him down, no mayor or governor could fire him, yet Robert Moses held the power throughout New York City and State to condemn housing, displace people, reshape the landscape, add highways, and build parks. He was soon the most prolific builder in Depression-weary America, with staggering amounts of money at his disposal.

^ Robert Moses, 1939

It worked wonders. New York City needed a bridge connecting Manhattan to the Bronx but lacked the funds to build it. Waiting for a federal loan or raising tax money during the Depression would take years. Thanks to his track record, Robert Moses's Triborough Authority raised over $5 million in ten weeks through bond issues, and built the Henry Hudson Bridge. The interest and amortization on those bonds cost $370,000 annually. If every car crossing the bridge paid 10 cents at the tollbooth, the Authority needed 3.7 million cars to meet the annual debt. In 1938, over 10 million cars crossed the Henry Hudson Bridge, in 1939 almost 13 million. Even with salaries and maintenance expenses, the revenue from that bridge was wildly success-ful, forcing the Authority to retire its forty-year bonds in less than a decade, issuing new ones while reaping millions annually to be spent on "any other corporate purpose." And that's just one bridge. Naturally, the Authority built six more. No New Yorker loved the automobile more than Robert Moses, and he didn't even drive.

^ The original Pennsylvania Station, 1962

Drunk with power, Moses took to the streets, building every major highway in New York, from Harlem River Drive to the Gowanus Expressway; sixteen in all, each providing more bonds and more toll money. With such success, banks were quick to make loans to the Authority. The federal government provided funds as well, for urban renewal projects and roadway developments, which the Triborough Authority spent throughout the city. For example, $180 million was spent to add one hundred thirty-two acres of landfill along Riverside Drive, creating Riverside Park and the West Side Highway. Upon its opening, the *Journal-American* pronounced the park "a fountain of health and pleasure;" the *Daily News* hailed the West Side Highway "the most beautiful drive in the world."

But not all of Moses' ideas met such praise. He angered many residents by demolishing magnificent Penn Station and shoehorning Madison Square Garden between an office tower and the basement railroad station. He overrode their fury as he constructed Park Avenue South, razing buildings and displacing people to extend Park Avenue down to Union Square. His next plan: do the same thing to Fifth Avenue, tearing up historic Washington Square and the center of Greenwich Village to create Fifth Avenue South, a tony address, he assured his detractors, which would attract luxury residential development and increased tax revenues. Village neighbors, known worldwide for their activism, gathered in protest. Meanwhile, Moses planned a Lower Manhattan Expressway, connecting the Holland Tunnel to the Williamsburg and Manhattan bridges, which would tear up Broome Street and destroy hundreds of historic cast-iron buildings. Uptown, he proposed to "renew" the west side between Central Park and Broadway by demolishing its brownstones, to be replaced by blocks of new high-rises.

However, the tide of public opinion officially turned against him on April 17, 1956, over an unlikely project: the parking lot at the Tavern On The Green. The Parks Commissioner planned to tear up a section of Central Park used by West Side mothers with pre-school children to provide more space for cars. Well-heeled and well connected, these mothers watched the arrival of surveyors and bulldozing equipment, then contacted the press. Within hours, radio stations were telling listeners of the mothers' success at facing down a bulldozer with their baby carriages. Evening news broadcasts on television confirmed the images, only to be repeated in the next morning's newspapers. Humiliated by a week of editorials decrying the "mothers' battle to keep the grassy, wooded section a haven for their children," on April 24, Moses counterattacked before dawn. He summoned a platoon of uniformed park rangers to protect the bulldozer operators as they destroyed Central Park trees at 3 a.m. The outraged press went wild, running front-page photos of weeping mothers physically restrained by policemen while ax-wielding workmen ravaged Central Park.

Courtroom upheavals dogged Moses and the Triborough Authority for years, as scandals were exposed involving organized crime, questionable finance, and inaccurate reporting. Commissioner Moses, who once held twelve posts simultaneously within the city and state, met his match when Governor Nelson Rockefeller installed his brother Laurence as Moses' state-wide replacement.

The Landmarks Preservation Commission was established in 1965 to ensure that New York would never lose another Penn Station. In 1969, Mayor John Lindsay designated Greenwich Village as the largest landmark district anywhere in the United States, followed by the formation of Friends of Cast-Iron Architecture in 1970, to protect the architecture of Soho. The dynamo who started his public-service career so promisingly saw it end as politicians sidelined his wild notions for the streets of New York. Three mayors needed decades to devise a safer system of checks and balances for developing and maintaining New York's infrastructure.

Still, the victory belongs to Robert Moses. No city on earth grew at New York's rate under his leadership. Urban planners from every major city in America sought his advice on contracts, designs, personnel, and finance, yet none could amass the volume of work Moses accomplished in service to New York. His bridges, beaches, parks, and parkways are a legacy to be used, enjoyed and admired for generations.

21-1	Proposed Lower Manhattan Expressway	21-5	Harlem River Drive
21-2	Tribrough Bridge	21-6	Riverside Park and West Side Highway
21-3	Madison Square Garden	21-7	The Original Penn Station
21-4	Lincoln Center	21-8	Tavern on the Green

CHAPTER 22

MANHATTAN HEARS THE BEAT

HOW A GROUP OF WRITERS CHANGED NEW YORK

America was thrilled when World War II ended. After all, the Boys were back; new chapters could begin in squeaky-clean suburbs as society attempted to dismiss inner-city squalor, the emerging drug trade, and rising racial tensions.

As prosperous whites moved away from Manhattan, the population of poor people increased; three hundred seventy-five thousand blacks arrived between 1940 and 1960, and the number of Puerto Rican immigrants quadrupled. During this transition, a group of radicals emerged with a decidedly different view of the postwar world, determined to explore America's underside and report their discoveries. From the intellectual pursuits at Columbia University and the carnal pursuits of Times Square and bohemian Greenwich Village, these outspoken writers gave birth to the Beat Generation, a movement that started in the streets of Manhattan but soon commanded the attention of an international audience.

‹ William S. Burroughs, Lucien Carr and Allen Ginsberg, 1953

The movement got off to a strange start when seventeen-year-old Columbia freshman Allen Ginsberg and fellow student Lucien Carr headed to 48 Morton Street to visit David Kammerer, Carr's former teacher from St. Louis. Ginsberg, contemplating his homosexual orientation in an era when such things could barely be whispered, wrote that he was "going down to the Village where all the fairies were. It was both romantically glorious, and at the same time frightening and frustrating." A week later, he and Carr headed back downtown to 69 Bedford Street to meet Carr's friend William S. Burroughs, another St. Louis native, a writer by day and bartender by night. Soon after, Carr introduced these friends to football-star-turned-college-dropout Jack Kerouac, who lived with his girlfriend near the Columbia campus. A life-altering twist created a bond that the friends never anticipated: After a night of drinking in the West End Bar on Broadway at 114th Street, Kammerer made a pass at his former student Carr in Riverside Park; Carr stabbed him twice in the heart with a Boy Scout knife, killing him. Kerouac hid the knife while Burroughs escorted Carr to the police. When Kammerer's body was found floating in the Hudson off 108th Street, Kerouac and Burroughs were arrested as material witnesses, Carr pleaded guilty to manslaughter and served two years in prison.

The lurid tale catapulted their names and faces onto the front pages of all seven of New York's daily newspapers. When Ginsberg submitted one chapter about the incident to his teacher, Columbia's dean expressly forbade him to write further. The message was plain: Kerouac, Burroughs, and Ginsberg didn't fit within America's wholesome vision of college boys. They were outlaws.

That wasn't a tough position for up-and-coming writers. The three soon shared an apartment together at 419 West 115th Street. With Burroughs as their leader they found excitement in Times Square, hanging out in all-night bars with jazz musicians and servicemen, as well as hustlers, junkies, and prostitutes. The trio shared the belief that great secrets lurked at America's heart, and that personal transcendence might be found if they dared to explore the nation's soul. While politicians touted America's new prosperity, declaring American life to be the standard to which the world should aspire, Ginsberg, Kerouac, and Burroughs were arriving at a different conclusion. Despite the nation's victories abroad, there were many battles to be waged at home, specifically minority rights, and later gay rights.

These young writers listened to the music of bebop, sampled marijuana and recreational drugs, and observed that a new world still largely underground was being born. In the streets of Manhattan, they presided over the first counterculture movement to have a major impact on America's popular culture.

Herbert Huncke, a junkie hustler they met in Times Square referred to them as "beat," meaning beat down, or wasted. Kerouac heard additional possibilities in the word "beat," referring to a new cadence for speech and writing, and the new rhythms of jazz. The authors' works gained recognition and publication at about the time Russia launched its Sputnik satellite into orbit. Noting the leftist leanings of Kerouac, Ginsberg, and Burroughs, one witty reviewer lifted the "nik" from Sputnik, referring to the writers as beatniks. The label came to define a movement as well as an entire generation and a Manhattan neighborhood.

That beatnik neighborhood, of course, was Greenwich Village, though the writers could only afford to live on its periphery. Ginsberg first maintained an apartment at 346 West 15th Street, where he wrote the poems for his book *Empty Mirror*. He frequented the San Remo bar at 93 MacDougal Street, which soon attracted avant-garde artists Jackson Pollock, Willem de Kooning, composer John Cage, choreographer Merce Cunningham and many others. Village bars and coffee houses near Washington Square exploited their presence, attempting to cash in on New York's beatnik scene.

What did the Beat writers accomplish that provoked such interest? They wrote in a new, direct way that has influenced writers ever since. William S. Burroughs wrote his acclaimed *Naked Lunch* by forging a new "cut-up" writing technique, forcing the reader to accept short phrases as complete thoughts, simulating a rapid-fire thought processes in printed form.

^ Times Square

Allen Ginsberg claimed that he heard a prophetic voice telling him to "cultivate the terror, get right into it." From that inspiration came *Howl*, a stream-of-consciousness poem about the discarded dreams and discarded people in America. At a gallery event, with Kerouac sitting on the floor tapping rhythms on a wine jug and chanting "Go, go, go," Ginsberg read *Howl* to instant and unanimous acclaim, the first work of the era to speak for the outcasts. As a result, poetry readings became emblematic gatherings across Greenwich Village. Upon publication, *Howl* was deemed obscene; Ginsberg's words were put on trial. Following a climactic defense, Ginsberg was vindicated in court; a living American poet was suddenly famous.

Jack Kerouac crisscrossed America by car for three years with his pal Neal Cassady, two modern swashbucklers risking adventure. Early in April 1951, Kerouac taped together rolls of twenty-foot long Japanese writing paper, then fed one end into his typewriter. Fueled by coffee and Benzedrine, he wrote of his adventures, taking little time to sleep. Kerouac finished *On The Road* by April 22nd: eighty-six thousand words on a one hundred and twenty-foot roll. Written as one single paragraph with almost no punctuation, the prose "comes at you just as the road comes at you." Blinded by the deviant characters the two antiheroes encounter, no publisher would touch the manuscript, fearing the scrutiny of Senator Joseph McCarthy's Un-American Activities Committee. Following *Howl*'s courtroom battle, Allen Ginsberg championed Kerouac's novel, which was finally published in 1957. It is hailed today as a modern masterpiece.

The Beat era ended in New York for two reasons. Ginsberg, Kerouac and Burroughs saw their works trivialized as mainstream America wrestled to accept their gritty material. By 1958, the Village was overrun by weekend beatniks in berets and goatees. This superficiality reached its zenith in Maynard G. Krebs, a beatnik character on TV's *Dobie Gillis*; he provided comic relief with no sting or relevance to the Beats' New Vision.

More importantly, the assassination of President John F. Kennedy proved the Beats' point: there were darker secrets lurking in white-bread America after all. That catalytic moment in 1963 pointed rebellious writers in a new direction: hippiedom, as hippies soon replaced beatniks in Washington Square with new issues to challenge. Ideas initiated by the Beat Generation exploded into a new social awareness felt around the world.

22-1	Columbia University	**22-6**	Times Square
22-2	David Kammerer's Apartment 48 Morton Street	**22-7**	Ginsberg writes *Empty Mirror* 346 West 15th Street
22-3	William S. Burroughs' House 69 Bedford Street	**22-8**	San Remo Bar 93 MacDougal Street
22-4	West End Bar Broadway at 114th St.	**22-9**	Washington Square Park
22-5	Kerouac/Burroughs/Ginsberg Apartment: 419 West 115 Street		

CHAPTER 23.

SOHO STORY

A NEIGHBORHOOD GROWS

The nineteenth-century cast-iron buildings that make up the neighborhood south of Washington Square were subjects of contention in the twentieth century. Their bumpy transition from a collection of grimy iron buildings into a chic Manhattan neighborhood is a story of determination.

By the 1950s and '60s, New Yorkers had just about forgotten the buildings south of Houston Street. Up in Greenwich Village, home to many successful artists, landlords pocketed top dollar as tenants squeezed into tiny apartments. A short walk away, a spacious industrial section sat fallow; its zoning required landlords to rent only to small businesses in need of workspace. However, most of the garment-related businesses that once populated the area had relocated their machinery to the West 30s decades earlier to escape the fire-prone wooden floors within those cast-iron buildings. Even Ladies' Mile packed up and moved to larger shops above 14th Street. South of Houston Street was Manhattan's forgotten enclave.

New York City's Planning Commissioner, Robert Moses, thought he had the solution: tear down the aging and unprofitable cast-iron buildings to make

‹ Broadway, north from Spring Street, 1898

way for a Lower Manhattan Expressway. He proposed that a highway cut through the heart of the neighborhood, on Broome Street, linking the Holland Tunnel with the Williamsburg and Manhattan bridges.

Meanwhile, the art scene was changing. Contemporary artists like Jackson Pollock and Mark Rothko sold paintings that were larger than some apartment walls. They required large spaces in which to create these works. Greenwich Village artists just couldn't afford to stretch huge canvases in tight spaces and meet those Village rents. They had to find a better space.

A generation later, artists like Donald Judd, Alex Katz, Jeff Koons, Jean-Michel Basquiat and David Salle landed south of Houston Street and famously went to work. The ambience seemed to breed success; soon everyone dreamed of life in an edgy Soho loft. Those pioneering artists provoked a firestorm that took decades to quell—as politicians, landlords, manufacturers, bureaucrats, lawyers and brokers flexed their muscles to assume control over the rediscovered neighborhood.

First, that highway proposal had to be defeated. When local artists joined forces with a group of preservationists including Jane Jacobs, James Marston-Fitch, and Margot Gayle, activists discovered a new synergy when tackling City Hall. The city government agreed to save its money and retract its highway plans.

The next glitch: to relocate south of Houston Street, artists had to sign commercial leases for large workspaces, foregoing the protection of rent control, the laws that govern how much the landlords could raise rents on residential units.

Artists would now live and work in a single flat, not unlike their forebears at the Tenth Street Studios some fifty years earlier; a radical concept to most New Yorkers. Despite the commercial zoning, landlords looked the other way, pleased to see their buildings occupied again, seldom warning artists that to sleep in a commercial space was a violation of the law. It became the personal expense of Soho pioneers to make those commercial lofts habitable; what an artist saved on rent went into long-term investments in kitchens, bathtubs, hot water tanks, and space heaters.

Unlike commercial tenants who moved from one address to another as rents and business evolved, artists brought their families and moved in to stay. Enterprising landlords saw their neighborhood's appeal among the avant garde and cashed in. When the commercial leases expired, renewals were offered sometimes at quadruple the initial rent. The artists were being priced out of the area they made desirable.

The artists joined forces and complained to the city government, as did the landlords, whose rent increases were perfectly legal. Longtime tenants who rented space for manufacturing complained bitterly too, for the higher rents would "drive them from the borough," taking employment opportunities elsewhere. Mayor John Lindsay stepped into the fray. Initially elected as a Republican, Lindsay might have been expected to support the landlord's position, since it was they who paid the real estate taxes on the buildings at stake. Instead, Lindsay simply counted heads. There were more tenants than landlords. He would maintain his popularity when seeking re-election by supporting the tenants against their landlords. In subsequent elections, Lindsay never ran for office again as a Republican.

^ Broadway, north from Prince Street, 1904

Cast-iron Architecture

In 1848 industrial inventor James Bogardus proposed a solution to New York City's "housing problem". While traveling in England, he became enamored of the cast-iron facades used in the construction of bridges, aqueducts and the interiors of market halls and libraries. Determined to introduce the concept in America, he specified that the exterior of his new factory at Duane and Centre streets in downtown Manhattan be made of identical, pre-cast metal panels fabricated by pouring liquid iron into shapely molds. In far less time than it took masons to build a standard exterior, these panels would then be bolted to a brick interior wall. Soon, Bogardus had two foundries working overtime casting these panels.

The introduction of cast iron revolutionized structural engineering. In traditional multi-story construction, the walls on the ground floor needed extra thickness to support the weight of the walls above. The taller the building, the thicker the walls were at street-level. Invariably, this was at the expense of otherwise-valuable retail space. Not so with cast iron. Buildings partially made of brick and paneled in cast-iron became slimmer, taller, airier and more spacious. Street floors were transformed into wide panes of glass interspersed with tall slender columns

that held up the buildings. Of course, the wide windows were perfect for displays of commercial goods; the term "window-shopping" came into vogue at this time.

Despite its practicality, cast-iron construction fell from grace with the arrival of steel. The invention of a metal even stronger than cast-iron caused architects to rethink basic construction concepts. Instead of relying on exterior walls of brick, stone, or iron to support a building, steel beams made a rigid interior superstructure possible, supporting enormous weight.

In the zeal to make the city taller, cast-iron buildings fell to the wrecking ball. Those that survived became derelicts once the old garment district moved uptown. In August 1973, passage of a local landmark preservation law led to the federally backed National Historic Landmark designation for Soho in June 1978. Today, one hundred and thirty-nine iron-front buildings on twenty-six city blocks of Soho and scattered buildings in TriBeCa represent the largest collection of cast-iron buildings in the world. A stroll along Mercer Street, Greene Street, lower Broadway or Lafayette Street looks much as it did one hundred years ago. Only the trees have been added.

To guarantee affordable lofts, Mayor Lindsay envisioned an artist's commune in Soho. To avoid displacing the manufacturers, Lindsay decided there was no need to change the zoning, since artists were technically "manufacturing" art. In 1971 he devised the Department of Cultural Affairs with Bess Myerson, the former Miss America, as its Commissioner, overseeing a new Artist-in-Residence (A.I.R.) District, which roughly encompassed Broadway to West Broadway, Houston Street to Canal Street. To live and work from a single unit in this prime district, residents had to prove they were artists, and secure an Artist-in-Residence Certificate from the Department of Cultural Affairs.

Pioneering art dealer Paula Cooper opened the first gallery in Soho in 1968 on Prince Street. Ivan Karp, a former director of the Leo Castelli Gallery opened O.K. Harris Gallery on West Broadway in 1969. Enormously successful and influential, Castelli opened a downtown branch of his gallery in 1971 at 420 West Broadway, a building that eventually housed multiple galleries, becoming one of the prime gallery venues in New York City. Not all of the artists he represented were thrilled. Roy Lichtenstein, Castelli recalled, "told me that nobody will ever go there."

To maintain its character, the neighborhood needed new artists. The affordability of living and working lofts would be preserved only as long as resident artists sold their lofts to other artists. That logic worked for a few years, while real estate prices remained stable. However, as the real estate boom of the early 1980s worked its magic, artists turned out to be just as profit-minded as their former landlords. Artists in residence could no longer afford to think of selling lofts for their modest acquisition costs because they couldn't afford the prices outside Soho. New artists would have to pay competitive market prices, or Soho would stagnate.

To acquire a certificate from the Department of Cultural Affairs, an artist needed to present a portfolio of work along with proof of income from art. Some non-artists, who didn't qualify for the certificate, built lofts in the triangle-below-Canal Street instead. That TriBeCa neighborhood delivered loft living to anyone willing to pay the price, as Soho denizens quickly recognized. With the city government restricting Soho resales to the certificate holders, TriBeCa became the desirable place, driving the price of a downtown loft. Such well-known artists as Keith Haring and Red Grooms bought lofts just beyond the A.I.R. District.

‹ The first cast-iron house in New York

Downtown Triangle Completes A Circle

The triangle of land below Canal Street has been known as TriBeCa since the 1970s, but it was called Washington Market for far longer, starting soon after the Civil War. The South Street Seaport on the East River was too small to accommodate America's rapidly expanding shipping industry, so business shifted to the Hudson River on Manhattan's West side, where more piers could meet the demands of the trade boom.

The city government supported the process by building its Retail Market, a block-square bourse between Fulton and Vesey Streets on West Street, filled with stalls for produce vendors. In 1869, when Commodore Vanderbilt erected a freight terminal for his New York Central Railroad at nearby Laight Street, the neighborhood was plainly defined as New York's export center. For decades, a pedestrian couldn't even see the expansive Hudson River, as freighters and steamships occupied every inch of the waterfront.

The Washington Market was a noisy, smelly, congested free-for-all, with trains overhead, trucks lurching toward tunnels and four ferry terminals, while vendors hawked their wares in the cold, salty air or beside all-night bonfires. By 1935, the industry within those several blocks accounted for a whopping twenty-two percent of the entire nation's export trade, equaling the trade statistics of Boston, Philadelphia, San Francisco, and Chicago combined. The speed at which goods could now travel within America, thanks to rapid freight trains, meant that dairy products that can easily spoil could be shipped quickly from this central hub.

When Charles "Lucky Lindy" Lindbergh crossed the Atlantic in an airplane, exporters witnessed their future. By the end of World War II, most industries had packed and moved to the close proximity of airfreight hangars. The ferries stopped, train tracks were dismantled, the terminals were closed, the City demolished the Retail Market, and an entire neighborhood disappeared.

And that was the best thing that could have happened. Rambling storehouses with high ceilings turn out to make terrific homes. With architecture similar to that of Soho, TriBeCa was ripe for expansion as loft living gained in popularity.

Non-artists in the late 1970s avoided the complications of the Artist-In-Residence process by renovating the mostly-empty warehouses just south of Soho, where free-market prices prevailed. Celebrities carved out fantasy lofts tucked away from uptown tour buses. World-class restaurants moved in, and families brought the joyful sounds of permanent residence. The Washington Market lives again.

^ [top] Washington Market, 1895. [bottom] West Washington Market, 1936

That's when things got ugly. The arcane legalities required to buy a Soho loft remained one of the New York City government's best-kept secrets. With civil servants determining who made art, the cutting-edge district was soon populated by people simply clever enough to beat the system. Wealthy professionals who were married to artists built Soho pleasure palaces thanks to the spouse's mediocre-but-certifiable attempts at art. Or the rental trick: non-artists bought a full floor, apportioned a small section of it to be rented to an artist and then developed the remainder for themselves. Actor Wesley Snipes, for example, moved into an artist's loft as a subtenant since acting wasn't recognized as an art by the Department of Cultural Affairs, despite Snipes' celebrated career. Every downtown broker can share a similar war story.

The Department of Cultural Affairs finally had to loosen its restraints. In the late 1980s, savvy developers realized that by selling lofts as condominiums, and fully disclosing that while the building was located within the A.I.R. District, they could sell to anyone willing to sign a waiver. This indemnified the seller from any action that might be taken by the Department of Cultural Affairs. In a cost-cutting gesture, Mayor Rudy Giuliani's administration significantly reduced the size of the Department, disbanding the panel that once scrutinized applicant portfolios.

The original artists of Soho watched their neighborhood evolve far beyond the original plan for an art community. Then they joyfully cashed the walloping checks from a newer generation who paid retail for the privilege of owning a small piece of Soho. The demand hasn't subsided. Visitors from around the world are attracted to the stylish boutiques and trendy clubs within historic buildings. Soho's once-grimy buildings, molded in iron, are now protected as national landmarks.

23-1	Paula Cooper Gallery (1968 until 1996) 96 Prince Street		**23-4**	First Cast-Iron Building Duane Street at Centre Street
23-2	OK Harris Gallery 383 West Broadway		**23-5**	South Street Seaport
23-3	Leo Castelli Gallery (1971 until 1999) 420 West Broadway		**23-6**	Retail Market West Street between Fulton and Vesey streets.
			23-7	New York Central Railroad Terminal: Laight Street

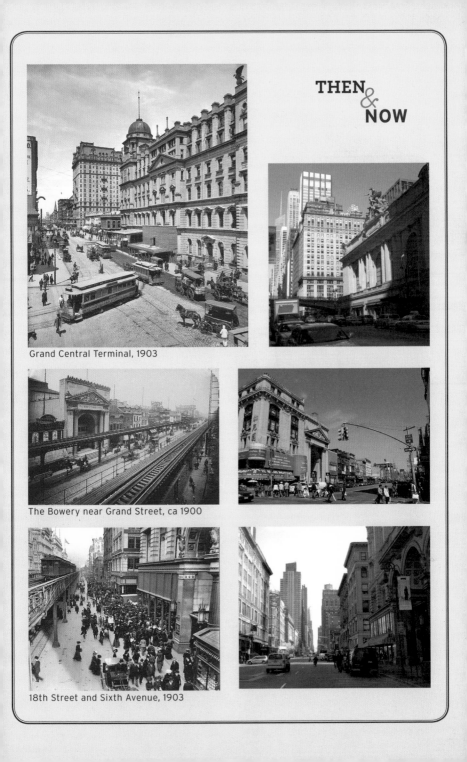

THEN & NOW

Grand Central Terminal, 1903

The Bowery near Grand Street, ca 1900

18th Street and Sixth Avenue, 1903

CHAPTER 24.

CHELSEA
WESTERN FRONTIER

When the popularity of Soho priced out artists and even
galleries in the 1990s, the creative crowd started looking west, to the spacious warehouses in the westernmost
reaches of Chelsea—the neighborhood west of Fifth Avenue bounded by 14th Street and 34th Street.

Along with the city's contemporary art scene, the neighborhood is now
home to popular nightclubs, high-end shopping and the city's new-media
corridor, the so-called Silicon Alley. But alongside Google and galleries,
some of Manhattan's richest history can be found in Chelsea.

Once the sprawling farm of Clement Clark Moore, author of *A Visit From
St. Nicholas*, the land was divided into city blocks in the early 1800s. The
Moores donated one block of their land to the Presbyterian Church, on
which it built the first seminary in America. Today the General Theological
Seminary occupies the land from Ninth Avenue to Tenth Avenue
from 20th to 21st streets, and serves as the centerpiece of the Chelsea
Landmark District.

‹ The Chelsea Hotel, 1936

Residents may stroll its rolling pastoral lawn, one of Chelsea's most romantic and best-kept secrets.

Along with its rich history, the area has long been home to a diverse population—from wealthy families to the punk-rock scene at the infamous Chelsea Hotel, once populated by the likes of Sex Pistols bassist Sid Vicious and his girlfriend Nancy Spungen, who met her untimely end at the hotel in 1978.

In the 1980s, when the Gay Men's Health Crisis opened its office on the ground floor of 318 West 22nd Street, Chelsea was already viewed as the largest enclave of gay men and lesbians in Manhattan, with many gay-friendly businesses that remain to this day.

The area's resurgence stems, in part, from new uses for the once-empty pier buildings along the river. They now serve as a film and television studio (for NBC's *Law & Order* among others), and Chelsea Piers, a huge sports complex including a skating rink and gymnastics center.

As Chelsea solidified its reputation as one of the city's cultural hotspots, world-class architects such as Frank Gehry made their mark on the neighborhood, creating a landscape that embraces the future without forgetting history. In 2009 the High Line opened, an innovative elevated greenway park fashioned from a formerly abandoned rail line. The park was a pet project for some of the area's boldface neighbors, including designer Diane von Furstenberg and actor Ethan Hawke. It has become a favorite among locals and tourists alike, as a prime place to view Chelsea's eclectic architectural past and present.

^ Clement Clark Moore

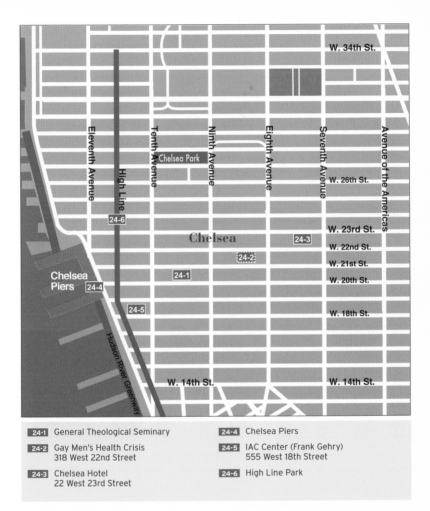

24-1 General Theological Seminary	**24-4**	Chelsea Piers
24-2 Gay Men's Health Crisis 318 West 22nd Street	**24-5**	IAC Center (Frank Gehry) 555 West 18th Street
24-3 Chelsea Hotel 22 West 23rd Street	**24-6**	High Line Park

CHAPTER 25

FATHERS AND SONS:
THE REAL ESTATE DYNASTIES OF NEW YORK

Days after George Washington took the Presidential oath, John Jacob Astor bought two lots on the Bowery for $625 cash. The profits he reaped were so alluring that future generations were groomed just to pass the torch. To most Americans in those days, Astor's first real estate transaction seemed like no bargain; after all, Peter Minuit supposedly bought the whole island of Manhattan for bunches of beads and $24 worth of Spanish-milled coins.

But to twenty-six-year-old Astor, that comparison clinched the deal: Manhattan's land values increased spectacularly, despite upheavals like the Revolution and the French and Indian War. To Mr. Astor, the profits from long term investments made Manhattan real estate a terrific family business.

‹ The GE building in Rockefeller Center, with Saint Patrick's Cathedral at the bottom left, 1933

Many other patriarchs dreamed of a real estate dynasty, though not all met with Astor's success or intergenerational continuity. Over the years, Astor invested thousands, acquiring undeveloped lots throughout Lower Manhattan. Meanwhile, those profitable investments financed Astor's son William through Germany's best universities, where he learned to manage and invest the family's portfolio. When William joined his father's Manhattan firm in 1830, the senior Astor was the wealthiest man in the New World, with $2 million in real estate holdings. Soon after, grandson John Jacob Astor III joined the family business too.

As New York's population exploded, Astor taught the merits of density to his descendants, collecting multiple rents from a single address. On a strawberry patch that was later to be known as the Lower East Side, the Astors erected hundreds of tenement houses, soon packed with tens of thousands of European immigrants. The profits from those multiple units provided the capital to build the family's biggest moneymaker of all: the Astor House hotel on Broadway near City Hall. With three hundred bedrooms at $2 per night, the daily profits from the luxurious hotel guaranteed permanence for the Astor dynasty. In his old age, when John Jacob deeded the hotel to William for "one Spanish-milled dollar, with love and affection," the Astor dynasty was conveyed between generations.

Outside the family, John Jacob Astor confided that his son William "will never make money, but he'll keep what he has." An accurate observation: During his years as head of the estate, William managed only to double its size, a growth rate of between two and three percent annually, compounded. The old man's insights characterized many other second-generation investors in dynasties to come: the nature of their tasks differed from the tasks of the founders. While John Jacob took great risks in Manhattan property and reaped an enormous fortune, that same fortune constrained William from being equally daring. The first Astor had nothing to lose; the second, everything.

The next generation of real estate moguls keenly observed the Astor family's path to success. As self-employed entrepreneurs, these new Americans took responsibilities for their successes or failures. They saved their cash to invest in income-producing properties for themselves and their future generations while New York continued to prosper.

One such character was A. E. Lefcourt, who made a living on the streets selling newspapers and shining shoes. While most paperboys were content with one route, the entrepreneurial Lefcourt secured additional jobs, then paid other boys to deliver the papers for him. As Lefcourt explained it, if he could sell shoe shines, he could sell anything. He soon became a salesman for a dress manufacturer. When the owner retired, Lefcourt bought the business, hired more salesmen, then diversified his assets into Manhattan real estate. Lefcourt knew the Lower East Side sweatshops first-hand; here, laborers risked their lives over primitive sewing machines that caused fires almost daily. Following the tragic Triangle Shirtwaist Company fire in 1911, which sent one hundred and forty-six girls leaping out of windows to die on the Greene Street sidewalk, Lefcourt built the first loft building north of 34th Street, then encouraged other "needle trades" to move into safer buildings as well. In 1923, he formed his own construction company, assembled the major block fronts on Broadway and Eighth Avenue from 36th to 39th streets, and built today's Garment District. As manufacturers abandoned the downtown lofts that are some of today's trendiest residential addresses, Lefcourt's pioneering vision saved lives and earned him a fortune.

Best of all, Lefcourt had a son. On the occasion of Alan's bar mitzvah, Lefcourt deeded him a $10 million building at 34th Street and Madison Avenue. But the dreams of dynasties don't always work as planned. Five years later, in October 1929, Lefcourt announced plans to build the world's tallest building at Broadway and 49th Street, just weeks before the stock market crashed, sinking the country into the Great Depression. By February 1930, the boy was dead. The grieving Lefcourt scrapped his plans and built a modest eleven-story building instead. Over the entrance of the so-called Brill Building, Lefcourt placed a head-and-shoulders bust of his young son. Though A. E. Lefcourt is remembered as a prolific builder, there would be no Lefcourt dynasty.

^ Firemen search for victims of the Triangle Shirtwaist Company fire, 1911

Some sons forego the dynasty to seek other opportunities. By the time Joseph P. Kennedy's career as Ambassador to Great Britain ended in 1941, he had amassed $30 million investing in Wall Street and Hollywood. With such a significant cash hoard, he easily secured bank loans at favorable rates and began to invest in real estate. Kennedy would buy a building for $1 million, mortgage it for eighty percent of its value at the low rate of four percent per year, reap six percent profit from its rents even before the building appreciated, then use the mortgage dollars as down payment on other properties. His timing and access to cash were ideal. He bought the corner of 51st Street and Lexington Avenue for $600,000, and sold it for nearly $4 million; the corner of 46th Street and Lexington Avenue, bought for $1.7 million, was sold not much later for nearly $5 million; the corner of 59th and Lexington Avenue, bought for $1.9 million with only $100,000 in cash was sold for $6 million. In one lucky decade, Joseph P. Kennedy tripled his fortune. And Kennedy, too, had sons. However, those sons, comparing their dad's career as a political ambassador against his activities as an investor, famously chose the former. Kennedy liquidated most of his real estate holdings in New York to concentrate his attention and encouragement to the political careers of his offspring.

Some sons surpass the achievements of the earlier generation, as is surely the case of Fred and Donald Trump. As the son of Swedish immigrants, Fred Trump trained as a carpenter. Working as a teenager to support his widowed mother, he built his first one-family house in Queens at age seventeen. During the Depression and World War II, Fred Trump completed twenty-five hundred homes for the Federal Housing Administration, and parlayed his knowledge of government contracts into subsidized housing complexes in Bensonhurst and Brighton Beach in Brooklyn. However, Fred

^ Joseph Kennedy, 1939

Trump was investigated twice by the FHA: once for borrowing more money to erect two complexes than it had cost to build them, then pocketing $1.6 million in dividends without FHA approval. (Trump was not alone. Norman Tishman faced a similar investigation in Rego Park.) A decade later, Trump was again scrutinized unfavorably, for contributing too generously to political officials as they sought re-election. As opposing candidates denounced his patronage, one politician was forced to resign from the city planning commission. Though the contributions were legal, laws were rewritten to prevent developers from getting too cozy with politicians.

Fred Trump's humiliation cemented young Donald's determination to get his father out of the subsidized housing industry and into prestigious projects. Soon after graduating from the University of Pennsylvania's esteemed Wharton School, he convinced his father to remortgage twenty-four thousand apartments, a move that provided cash for the younger Trump's expansion. For the next five years, Donald bought and sold apartment complexes, building equity, then made an audacious move into Manhattan, striking a deal with the near-broke Penn Central Railroad.

It was Donald who taught Fred the value of high-profile transactions as he acquired the Commodore Hotel adjacent to Grand Central Terminal. Paying $10 million, Donald gained the government's concession of no property taxes for forty years. He then turned the dilapidated building into the sleek Grand Hyatt hotel, following the lead of the earliest Astors.

^ John D. Rockefeller and son John D. Rockefeller, Jr., 1915

The publicity generated by that transaction was the attention for which Donald clamored. Soon he was being chauffeured around town like a movie star, socializing among the glitterati, reinventing the Trump name and establishing a dynasty as colorful as the Astors. Today, Trump is known across America for luxurious housing, and perhaps even more for his frequent television and tabloid appearances.

The most pensive lesson about a dynasty comes from the Rockefellers. After John D. Rockefeller, Sr., made his fortune in oil, his son John Jr. and grandson Nelson took great interest in developing today's Rockefeller Center, acres of real estate that are collectively hailed as one of Manhattan's greatest jewels. But within the Rockefeller dynasty, the steady income from the Center's investment proved insufficient, as subsequent generations stretched the family fortune to its limits. As the eighty-eight sons and daughters of Rockefellers dreamed their own entrepreneurial dreams, many inherited too little seed money to bring their ideas to fruition.

Making headline news on November 1, 1989, the fiftieth anniversary of Rockefeller Center, the dynasty sold its controlling interest to the Mitsubishi Company of Tokyo for $846 million. The sale deposited a huge cash infusion into the trusts from which the fifth-generation Rockefellers derive their income, empowering the youngest investors to realize their dreams.

The sale signaled the end of the Rockefeller's clout within Manhattan real estate, but opened exciting new doors. No longer constrained to maintaining the single fortune, the youngest generation scattered to begin their own dynasties, using the power of their family name to take new risks in multiple directions. And for that, Peter Minuit, John Jacob Astor, and fathers everywhere must share a knowing smile.

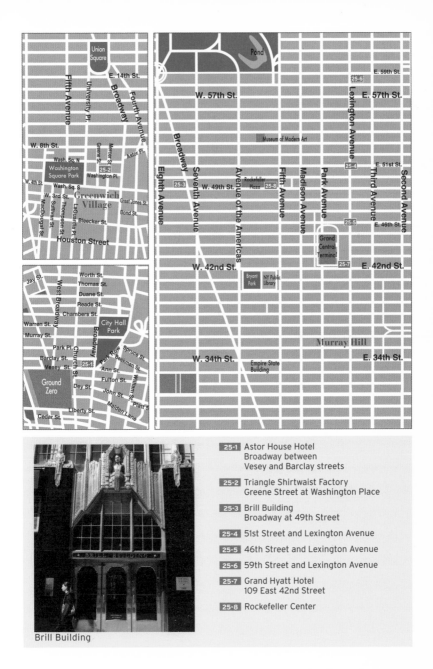

Brill Building

25-1 Astor House Hotel
Broadway between
Vesey and Barclay streets

25-2 Triangle Shirtwaist Factory
Greene Street at Washington Place

25-3 Brill Building
Broadway at 49th Street

25-4 51st Street and Lexington Avenue

25-5 46th Street and Lexington Avenue

25-6 59th Street and Lexington Avenue

25-7 Grand Hyatt Hotel
109 East 42nd Street

25-8 Rockefeller Center

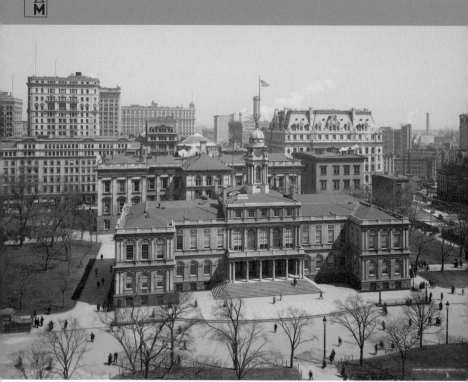

City Hall, 1904

FINANCIAL DISTRICT

An epic chapter was added to the already plentiful history of Lower Manhattan when the World Trade Center was attacked and destroyed on September 11, 2001. This walking tour circles the evolving construction site of the former World Trade Center as well as the historic streets that surround it, with anecdotes stretching back to America before the Revolutionary War. It's one of the earliest settlements in America.

Tour Time: about 3 hours
This Tour Contains Chapters: 1, 2, 5

START:
City Hall (260 Broadway)

SUBWAYS:
2 **3** to Park Place
A **C** to Broadway-Nassau
J **Z** to Fulton Street
R to City Hall
4 **5** **6** to Brooklyn Bridge

END:
Fraunces Tavern (54 Pearl Street)

SUBWAYS:
2 **3** at Wall Street
J **Z** at Broad Street
R at Whitehall Street
4 **5** Bowling Green

1. Start at the Eastern side of New York's City Hall, completed in 1812. It's a national landmark bounded by four curving streets: Broadway, Chambers Street, Park Row and Centre Street.

2. On the Centre Street side (the eastern side) of City Hall, notice the footpath that leads across the Brooklyn Bridge. After the American Revolution, New York City was America's first capital. The first executive mansion, occupied by George Washington, once stood right here but was demolished to build the Brooklyn Bridge ramp that now connects Manhattan to Brooklyn.

3. Walk south (downtown) as Centre Street curves around City Hall. This has been the site of many celebrations and protests. Walk past the intersection of Spruce Street, where Centre Street becomes Park Row, for the best view of City Hall.

4. At the corner of Park Row and Broadway, across from City Hall, is the Woolworth Building. One of the most successful examples of early high-rise construction. The Woolworth Building was the tallest building on earth when it opened in 1913 (the Chrysler Building surpassed it in 1930); it still remains one of the twenty tallest buildings in New York. The luxurious Astor House Hotel once stood here, on Broadway between Barclay and Vesey streets.

5. Cross Broadway toward the Woolworth Building; notice on the other side of Broadway is Barclay Street. Continue walking straight ahead on Barclay Street to the corner of Church Street, then turn left (south).

6. It's here that you'll encounter your first view of the tragic World Trade Center site. This tour will view three sides of Ground Zero. Continue walking south on Church Street.

7. At the corner of Church Street and Vesey Street, turn left (east), walking away from Ground Zero. Near the middle of the block, visit the 9/11 Memorial Preview Site at 20 Vesey Street, which shows architectural models and explains the construction currently under way. Admission is free; the exhibit opens at 10 a.m. every day.

8. Cross Vesey Street to enter the cemetery behind Saint Paul's Chapel, the oldest building in continuous use in New York City. Built in 1766, it is the only colonial church still standing in Manhattan.

9. Stroll through the cemetery then enter the chapel. President George Washington worshipped here on his Inauguration Day and during the years of his presidency. Some of America's first colonists from the 1700s are buried in its historic graveyard. More recently, Saint Paul's Chapel served as a temporary refuge for heroic recovery workers digging through the rubble following the 9/11 disaster. Its graveyard was completely covered with inches of ashes from the collapsed Twin Towers. The interior of Saint Paul's Chapel now overflows with warm wishes from around the world in memory of the September 11th attacks.

10. Exit the chapel through the same entrance door, strolling again through the cemetery.

11. Turn to the left (south) to exit the cemetery grounds, then turn right on Fulton Street, walking again toward Ground Zero.

12. At the opposite side of the construction site stands the World Financial Center. It too was severely damaged during the 9/11 attacks, with the all-glass Winter Garden almost completely demolished. Today, all has been restored; open to the public, its lobbies are the ideal vantage point for views of construction activity on the World Trade Center site.

13. At the corner of Fulton Street and Church Street, turn left (south). Walk three blocks down Church Street to Liberty Street, along the eastern perimeter of Ground Zero.

14. At the corner of Liberty Street, turn right (west) to walk toward the covered walkway that guides visitors into the World Financial Center lobby.

15. On the way, you'll pass the Tribute WTC Visitor Center at 120 Liberty Street. It documents the emotional history of the 9/11 disaster and recovery, as well as the site's future plans. Admission is $10.

16. Continue walking west on Liberty Street to the covered walkway. Follow the signs to the stairs (and elevator) that lead visitors up one flight to the lobby of One World Financial Center.

17. The glass-lined corridor provides the best vantage point for photos of Ground Zero devastation and construction. Continue walking west, through the revolving doors, inside One World Financial Center. (After observing and photographing the Ground Zero site, you may skip to step 22 and shorten your visit by returning through the corridor and back to Liberty Street.)

18. In the spacious lobby of One World Financial Center, follow the windows along the Ground Zero site. From these windows, visitors can appreciate the scale of the disaster that occurred here, but also witness the resilient spirit of New Yorkers who restored the salvageable buildings that surround it.

19. Continue to the right (north) through the lobby to the revolving doors at Two World Financial Center; Ground Zero is no longer in view. Follow the indoor signs that lead to the Winter Garden.

20. The vaulted glass ceiling over the Winter Garden was completely demolished in the devistation of 9/11. Today, its splendor has returned (palm trees are a rare sight in Manhattan!). Walk down to sea level on the marble stairs (or, take the escalator at the western end), and step outside for a view of the Hudson River and yacht basin. The outdoor cafés are open daily (weather permitting) for lunch and dinner.

21. Stroll to the left (south) through the panoramic garden along the Hudson River. Near the southern end of the garden, enter again into One World Financial Center. An escalator whisks visitors back to the upper lobby level.

22. Exit the World Financial Center by retracing your steps through the lobby and corridor that leads back to Liberty Street. Use the stairs (or elevator) to return to the Liberty Street sidewalk.

23. Walk straight ahead on Liberty Street, past the open plaza, directly to Broadway.

24. At the corner of Liberty Street and Broadway, turn right (south), heading into the heart of the Financial District.

25. A short distance down Broadway, you'll come to Trinity Church, New York's first Episcopal church. Although its original charter was issued by King William III of England in 1697, its colonial parishioners were more interested in severing their ties with England. Members of the First and Second Continental Congresses worshipped here, and one signer of the Declaration of Independence—Francis Lewis—is buried in the historic cemetery.

26. Trinity Church also stand at the apex of Wall
Street, named for the long wall that early
Dutch settlers built here to protect themselves
from attacks by the various Native American
tribes that populated Manhattan island.

27. Turn to the left, cross Broadway, and stroll east
on Wall Street. You'll pass a private entrance to
the New York Stock Exchange (11 Wall Street,
on the right). Continue straight ahead and plan
to spend a few minutes in the public square at
the intersection of Wall Street and Broad Street,
where you'll find a better view of the NYSE.

28. This is one of the most famous intersec-
tions in American history, for here is Federal
Hall, America's original Capitol. You're standing where the first Americans stood as they
witnessed the Inauguration of America's first
President, George Washington, in 1789. The Bill
of Rights was signed into law here in 1791.

29. Admission to Federal Hall is free. Among the
displays inside is President Washington's
handwritten Inaugural Address, which
he delivered to the U.S. Senate.

30. To continue the tour, notice that on the western
side of Federal Hall, Broad Street's name changes
to Nassau Street. Walk north on Nassau Street,
beside Federal Hall toward Pine Street.

31. Turn right (east) on Pine Street, along
the back wall of Federal Hall.

32. At the corner of Pine and William streets, you'll see
the very modern headquarters for Chase Bank at
One Chase Manhattan Plaza. The modern sculpture,
entitled Four Trees, created by Jean Dubuffet, was
acquired by David Rockefeller for the Chase Bank.

33. From inside the plaza, turn left (west),
heading back toward Nassau Street.

34. On Nassau Street, turn right (north). The building on the corner of Liberty and Nassau streets that looks like a fortress is the Federal Reserve. Built in 1924, this landmark building houses more gold bars than even Fort Knox. The gold stockpile rests in vaults five stories underground, safely embedded in Manhattan's solid bedrock.

35. Turn to the right (east), and walk along the front of the Federal Reserve. At the corner of William Street, turn right (south) to walk along the border of Chase Manhattan Plaza.

36. The opulent towers erected on these narrow streets are bastions to finance, built by banks that no longer exist. At the corner of Wall Street, turn left.

37. On the north side, 48 Wall Street once housed The Bank of New York, but is now the Museum of American Finance. Across the street, 55 Wall Street was the site of the original Merchants Exchange, a forerunner to the New York Stock Exchange. It later became headquarters for Citibank (formerly known as First National City Bank). The bankers retained architect Stanford White to double the size of the building, adding its present facade of Corinthian columns. No longer a bank, this historic site now houses restaurants and condominiums.

38. At the end of the block, turn right (south) onto Hanover Street. Walk one block to the corner of Exchange Place and turn right (west) to observe 20 Exchange Place, a skyscraper from 1930. When First National City Bank merged with Farmers' Loan and Trust (the predecessor to Citigroup), this was the corporate headquarters. It's now a New York City landmark, and still one of its tallest buildings.

39. Walk to the corner of Exchange Place and William Street, then turn left and keep walking south. At the next intersection, follow South William Street as it curves southwestward. During the city's first

years, this side of Wall Street was occupied by Dutch settlers who called the area Nieuw Amsterdam.

40. Walk along picturesque South William Street to the corner of tiny Mill Lane. Turn left and walk through Mill Lane to the historic Stone Street landmark district.

41. At Stone Street, turn to the right and follow this curving street, which is reputed to be the first in New York City that was paved (with cobblestones) by the Dutch circa 1658. Although the Dutch called it High Street, the British called it Duke Street, in honor of the Duke of York. After the American Revolution, there were no more honors for British dukes, and the place was renamed Stone Street in 1794. The early buildings were destroyed in a fire in 1835, replaced by these "counting houses" (as accounting offices were once called). The facades and sidewalks were restored in the 1990s.

42. Follow Stone Street to its end, where it intersects with Pearl Street. Then turn right (west) to walk one more block along Pearl Street. Before New York Harbor was built, when tides lapped against the sandy beach nearby, this street was known as Mother-of-Pearl Street for the shiny shells that were frequently discovered here.

43. Stop at the corner of Pearl and Broad streets, the site of Fraunces Tavern, founded as the Queen's Head Tavern in 1762 and later run by Samuel Fraunces. At the end of the American Revolution, it was here on the second floor that General George Washington dismissed his commanders. The war with Britain was over; an independent nation was born. Not a moment for celebration, this was the site of Washington's famous and solemn farewell.

44. Fraunces Tavern is a national landmark but also a functioning restaurant, a great place to raise a glass and toast the sprawling history of New York City.

Fraunces Tavern, 1904

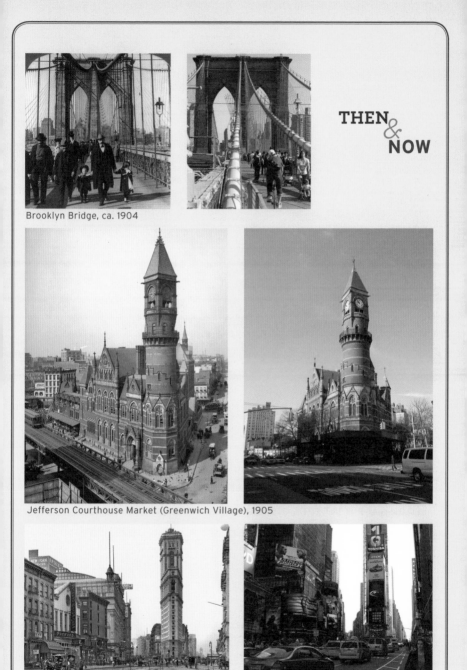

THEN & NOW

Brooklyn Bridge, ca. 1904

Jefferson Courthouse Market (Greenwich Village), 1905

Longacre Square (Times Square), 1904

Mulberry Street, 1900

CHINATOWN / SOHO

Since New York's first residents settled in the lower region of the island of Manhattan, this area's history is rich. Today, it's a vibrant display of many cultures, proving New York's moniker as "the great melting pot." This walk winds through four distinct neighborhoods.

Tour Time: about 2.5 hours
This Tour Contains Chapters: 7, 18, 21, 22, 23

START:
Information Kiosk at
Baxter Street at Canal Street

SUBWAYS:
6 to Canal Street
J Z to Canal Street
N Q R to Canal Street
B D to Grand Street

END:
Washington Square

SUBWAYS:
B D F M or **A C E**
at West 4th Street
N R at 8th Street/NYU
6 at Astor Place

1. Start at the Official NYC Information Kiosk at the intersection of Baxter and Canal streets.

2. Walk south (right) on Baxter Street until you arrive at Columbus Park, at the corner of Bayard Street. Continue walking along the park, until Baxter Street meets Worth Street; Cross Street (now Mosco Street) once met here as well. Before the Civil War, this was New York's worst slum (as depicted in Martin Scorsese's film *Gangs of New York*), an area called Five Points (for all these intersecting streets) populated primarily by Irish toughs.

3. There are no traces of Five Points any longer; those buildings were demolished, street patterns revised and Chinese settlers moved in when the Irish moved out. But use your imagination to picture Paradise Square and the infamous Old Brewery, long since buried under the New York State Supreme Court building at 60 Centre Street.

4. Walk east (left) to Chatham Square—also known as Kimlau Square—where Worth Street, Saint James Street, Park Row, and Mott Street all converge in one confusing intersection.

5. Follow Mott Street as it curves uptown (north), considered by many to be the "Main Street" of Manhattan's Chinatown. Most longtime residents are of Cantonese descent, but in later years a new dialect arrived from Hong Kong. Unlike the gentrified

Chinatowns in other American cities, New York's Chinatown is a place for immigrants to get a new start. It's the rare place where you'll find Hong Kong, Vietnamese, Cantonese, Szechuan and Mandarin restaurants beside fish markets and herbalists, as well as contemporary fashions and art galleries.

6. Continue the stroll up Mott Street to Canal Street. Turn left (west) on Canal Street, a very busy shopping street.

7. Walk one block, to Mulberry Street. Turn right (north), crossing Canal Street to walk up Mulberry Street.

8. Canal Street is the abrupt dividing line between Chinatown and the neighborhood known as Little Italy. Here you'll find blocks of Italian culture, from large restaurants to tiny espresso cafés and pastry shops.

9. Continue walking north on Mulberry Street.

10. At the corner of Mulberry Street and Grand Street, consider a sweet diversion just a few paces to the right (east). Ferrara Bakery and Café (195 Grand Street) has been a neighborhood institution since 1892, providing pastries to some local restaurants as well as catering some opulent weddings. Stop in for a gelato or cannoli to enjoy as your stroll continues.

11. Walk north on Mulberry Street through the streets of Little Italy. Although mafia characters in *The Godfather* and *The Sopranos* are pure fiction, their real-life counterparts, the Five Families that control organized crime, have historically called this neighborhood home. Mafia "rub-outs" are rare, but not uncommon, here.

12. For example, at the corner of Mulberry Street and Broome Street, you'll pass Umberto's Clam House. Shortly after Mafia don Joe Colombo was shot, Joey Gallo—the prime suspect in the Colombo shooting—was shot in gangland style at Umberto's Clam

House in 1972. The restaurant relocated to this corner, but hasn't shed its colorful reputation.

13. Take a moment to look up and down Broome Street. In the early 1960s, Robert Moses proposed a Lower Manhattan Expressway that would connect the Holland Tunnel with the Williamsburg and Manhattan bridges. The planed eight-lane highway would have displaced nearly two thousand residents and destroyed historic buildings and businesses along fourteen blocks in Soho and Little Italy. Thanks to the work of preservationists led by activist Jane Jacobs, the plan was defeated in 1964, and the neighborhood retains its historic charm.

14. Continue walking north on Mulberry Street. You'll soon notice a change in the neighborhood again, as you approach an area that real estate brokers call NoLIta (for North Of Little Italy). Continue on Mulberry Street to the corner of Spring Street.

15. Turn left (west) onto Spring Street, a busy shopping street on the edge of Soho.

16. Stay on Spring Street, but look to your left, down Lafayette Street to view the ornate Police Building, built in 1909 as the NYPD headquarters. When the Police Department moved out in 1973, the building became a New York City landmark. Due to the city's chronic housing shortage, many large commercial buildings in this area have been converted to residential use including the Police Building, which became fifty-five spacious condominiums in 1988.

17. Continue walking west on Spring Street.

18. At the corner of Broadway, turn right (north) and stroll along busy Broadway for one block. These buildings were built for the garment industry and light manufacturing, but today many of these floors are lofts where artists live and work instead.

19. Stop at the corner of Prince Street to note two famous buildings. The Singer Sewing Machine Company is a New York City landmark, built in 1902. (Singer promptly outgrew this place and built much larger headquarters on Liberty Street in 1908.) In the 1970s, this building became one of the first manufacturing buildings on Broadway to be converted into residential lofts. Shaped like an "L", you'll see more of the building around the corner on Prince Street.

20. Stay on this corner to observe another kind of history. On the northwest corner of Broadway and Prince Street, the loft on the second floor of 565 Broadway is the site of MTV's first season of *The Real World*, a program that many people consider the original reality television show. The building has undergone some renovations and the neighborhood is far more populous than it was in those 1992 broadcasts, but this is the place that launched hopes and heartbreaks, and many entertainment careers.

21. Cross Broadway, heading west on Prince Street. This area is a New York City landmark district, not for the unique interiors of artists' lofts above, but for the rare exterior facades made of cast-iron. The Soho Cast-Iron District spans twenty-six city blocks and includes about five hundred buildings.

22. At the corner of Greene Street, turn right (north) to see an entire block of cast-iron buildings on a cobblestone street. Fitting these large panels of cast-iron together to form an exterior facade enabled developers to erect buildings rapidly. Most buildings in the Soho Cast-Iron District were built in the decades shortly before and after the Civil War. The construction process fell out of favor with the invention of steel, an even stronger material that made New York's skyscrapers possible. No longer used for manufacturing, all of these buildings are now live/work lofts.

23. Keep walking north on Greene Street. Soho (and the Cast-Iron Landmark District) officially end at Houston Street.

24. From Greene Street, cross to the north side of Houston Street, heading toward some modern high-rise apartments known as the Silver Towers. This is faculty housing built by New York University, with a surprise in its center.

25. Turn left (west) and walk a short distance to the corner of Wooster Street, then turn right (north) to enter the apartment complex, which was designed by architect I.M. Pei.

26. In the center you'll discover a giant sculpture by Pablo Picasso. Entitled *Bust of Sylvette*, it was a gift to New York University in 1968.

27. Walk past the sculpture then turn to the left (west) to exit.

28. Walking down the steps that lead from the university apartments, you'll be on LaGuardia Place, home of the late artist Keith Haring.

29. Turn to the right (north) and walk to the corner of Bleecker Street.

30. Turn left (west) and cross LaGuardia Place to explore Bleecker Street, the home of beatniks in the 1950s and early 1960s. Some of the beatniks' historic coffee houses still stand, although the neighborhood has evolved around them.

31. At 147 Bleecker Street, you'll find The Bitter End, where an extraordinary list of performers got their starts, including Bob Dylan, Joan Baez, Billy Joel, Jackson Browne, Joni Mitchell, George Carlin, Judy Collins, Bill Cosby, Pete Seeger, James Taylor, and many more.

32. Keep walking west on Bleecker Street until you reach MacDougal Street; then turn right (north).

33. The coffee houses from the Beat Generation continue here, although many have evolved to suit new tastes over the decades. Walk north on MacDougal Street, past unique mom-and-pop shops for food and clothing.

34. Near the middle of the block, stop at the intersecting street called Minetta Lane. At that corner, you'll find Café Wha, another Beat Generation establishment with an astounding list of performers. Even older than The Bitter End, Café Wha was a regular hangout for poet Allen Ginsburg, a long-time resident of Greenwich Village. Performers who launched their careers here include: Bob Dylan, Jimi Hendrix, Bruce Springsteen, Kool and the Gang, and Peter, Paul & Mary, to name a few. But don't let the venue's website fool you, the original Café Wha was next door at 117 MacDougal. The owner, Manny Roth, uncle to David Lee Roth, sold the original property in 1988; it is now the Comedy Cellar.

35. Stay on MacDougal Street and continue walking north. At the corner of Washington Square, turn right (east). The brick building on this corner is the law school for New York University, the place where longtime New Yorker John F. Kennedy, Jr., famously earned his law degree.

36. Cross the street to enter Washington Square Park, the epicenter of Greenwich Village, and a colorful place to relax.

Grove Street, 1936

GREENWICH VILLAGE

Greenwich Village was once a bucolic suburb of New York City. Since then, artists, activists, beatniks and bohemians have all called it home. This tour starts at Washington Square Park, the center of it all, and explores the neighborhood's uniquely winding streets, built before the grid system was adopted.

Tour Time: about 3.5 hours
This Tour Contains Chapters: 3, 4, 5, 19, 24

START:
Washington Square

SUBWAYS:
(B) (D) (F) (M) or (A) (C) (E)
to West 4th Street
(N) (R) to 8th Street/NYU
(6) to Astor Place

END:
The High Line

SUBWAYS:
(L) or (A) (C) (E) at 14th Street
(1) (2) (3) at 14th Street

1. From the Washington Square Arch, facing Fifth Avenue, turn to the left and walk west. The street name of Washington Square North changes to Waverly Place (Note: Greenwich Village streets were determined before Manhattan's grid pattern was adopted. Be prepared for circuitous streets that don't conform to true east and west. That's part of Greenwich Village's charm.)

2. Continue walking west on Waverly Place, past Sixth Avenue, also known as Avenue of the Americas.

3. Notice the curbstones at the sidewalk's edge on either side of Waverly Place. That stone doesn't exist anywhere else on this continent. These hewed curbstones originally served as ballast in the hulls of English ships heading to New York, then a British colony. You'll see these non-indigenous gray curbstones throughout almost all streets in Greenwich Village west of Sixth Avenue.

4. Turn to the right (north). Cross the intersection of Waverly Place and Christopher Street near the triangular Christopher Park, then walk to 53 Christopher Street. A famous Civil Rights protest occurred at this bar in July 1969, when New York City Policemen arrived at midnight at the Stonewall Inn to harass its gay patrons and shake down the management for graft. It was an all-too-common occurrence, but this time a bottle went flying as gay men fought back against the police.

The melee continued for three days, as more gays from around the Village battled against the cops indoors and around the park across the street. Gay people everywhere acknowledge the Stonewall Rebellion as the beginning of the international gay rights movement. The Stonewall Inn was completely destroyed (though it's reopened under new management bearing little resemblance to the original).

5. Walk west to the corner of Christopher Street, then turn left and cross the street onto the triangular park. Enter the park from its Seventh Avenue side. A sculpture of two gay couples, created by sculptor George Segal, quietly commemorates the famous protest of 1969 and its loving aftermath.

6. Exiting the park, walk a few paces south to return to Waverly Place. Cross Seventh Avenue, where the street's name changes to Grove Street.

7. Once the site of Thomas Paine's home, 59 Grove Street is where you'll find Marie's Crisis Café, which served as a brothel and bar during the 19th century. During prohibition it was a popular speakeasy.

8. Continue walking west on Grove Street, noting the ironwork in front of these houses. Since they were built before roads were paved, you'll see an occasional shoe scraper built into the original ironwork near the lower steps on these stoops. You're viewing some of the oldest houses still standing in America.

9. Grove Street is a typical tree-lined street in Greenwich Village. Streets like this one extend to the north and south; they've provided homes for generations of notable Americans, including playwright Eugene O'Neill, activists John Reed, Louise Bryant and Emma Goldman, actors Bette Midler, Sarah Jessica Parker and Matthew Broderick, and many, many more.

10. Continue walking on Grove Street to the corner of Bedford Street, then turn left (south).

11. A few paces from the corner of Bedford and Commerce streets, you'll see the smallest house in New York at 75 1/2 Bedford Street. Once the home of poet Edna St. Vincent Millay, the tiny house is just ten feet wide; it sold in 2010 for just over $2 million.

12. From Bedford Street, turn west onto Commerce Street. It's the site of the Cherry Lane Theatre, off-Broadway's first theater, founded by Edna St. Vincent Millay and friends in 1924. It's the home of many theatrical successes, including the original productions of *Godspell*, *Nunsense*, *True West*, T*o Be Young, Gifted and Black*, *Little Mary Sunshine*, and many more.

13. Follow the curve of Commerce Street to where it intersects again with Barrow Street. Turn right (east) onto Barrow Street, back to Bedford Street. At the corner of Bedford Street, turn left (north) and walk for one block to the corner of Grove Street.

14. On the Northeast corner of Bedford Street and Grove Street stands one of the last remaining wooden houses in all of New York City.

15. The Tudor house next door at 102 Bedford Street has been home to several famous actors, including Errol Flynn and Charles Laughton.

16. Turn left (west) onto Grove Street. Halfway down the block, the street curves. On the south side of the street, look for the wrought-iron gate that permits a peek at Grove Court, a collection of tiny private houses with a common garden in front, one of Greenwich Village's most charming and historic addresses.

17. Continue walking down Grove Street to Hudson Street. When Vice President John Adams lived in Greenwich Village, the Hudson River actually lapped against the shore here, but as the city's hills were flattened, landfill was added to make way for additional streets to the west. Directly ahead, on that landfill on the western side of Hudson Street stands Saint Luke in the Fields Church.

18. Since Greenwich Village's population grew as residents from the congested area near today's Financial District relocated here, the churches relocated, too. Saint Luke's Church was built as an extension of the Trinity Church parish further downtown. Its tiny Meditation Garden is often open to the public. Enter from Hudson Street.

19. Turn right and walk north on Hudson Street to Christopher Street, one of the major shopping streets of Greenwich Village. Turn right (east) onto Christopher Street, where you'll pass the Lucille Lortel Theatre. Known for decades as the Theatre de Lys, it proved the viability of off-Broadway by presenting *The Threepenny Opera* (which ran for seven years!) with Lotte Lenya, John Astin, Paul Dooley, and the very young Beatrice Arthur among its original cast. This theater launched many shows that moved to larger quarters uptown on Broadway.

20. Continue to walk east on Christopher Street, where you'll find many quaint shops, including McNulty's Coffee and Tea Co., at 109 Christopher Street, a Village institution since 1895.

21. Walk to the corner of Bleecker Street, then turn left to view more scenic streets of Greenwich Village. Notice that the street signs are color-coded. Blocks with historic significance have brown signs; blocks not protected by landmark status have green street signs.

22. Walk North for two blocks on Bleecker Street, then turn right (east) onto Charles Street to observe the residential architecture. The heavy cornices at the tops of these buildings are made of cast-iron to protect the buildings from inclement weather at the vulnerable junction where the flat roof meets the front facade. The building at 74 Charles Street was the New York home of songwriter Woody Guthrie. Author Sinclair Lewis lived across the street, at 69 Charles Street.

23. At the corner of West 4th Street, turn left (north) and walk one block to the corner of Perry Street.

24. Turn left (west) onto Perry Street to savor the diverse architecture of Greenwich Village, from apartment buildings to elegant one-family houses; they all comprise one of America's largest landmark districts.

25. On Perry Street, cross Hudson Street, then turn right (north) and walk along the west side of Hudson Street. You'll soon encounter The White Horse Tavern, one of the oldest pubs in America, a place frequented by Welsh author and poet Dylan Thomas. He set a record here, downing eighteen whiskies in one night—then died the next morning.

26. At the corner of West 11th Street, turn left (west) and walk to the Hudson River. Cross Washington Street, the cusp of the landmark district. The buildings between here and the Hudson River are newly constructed condominiums or converted warehouses from the era when freighters lined the (now-demolished) piers along the river. Some of the residents in this modern area include actors Harrison Ford, Calista Flockhart and Nicole Kidman; the buildings are designed by some of the world's most celebrated architects, including Richard Meier and Frank Gehry.

27. Cross West Street to enter Henry Hudson Park. It's a great place for people watching, for relaxing, for a snack, or for a stroll along the Hudson River in either direction.

28. Then, turn around and walk back (east) to Washington Street.

29. At Washington Street, turn left (north) to visit more history.

30. Greenwich Village ends where the Meatpacking District begins, just north of West 12th Street. It's where butchers once packaged freshly slaughtered meats, where animal blood was not an uncommon sight on

the cobblestone streets. Today the neighborhood is a vibrant collection of boutiques and restaurants (as frequently seen in HBO's *Sex and the City*).

31. At Washington Street and Gansevoort Street, climb the stairs (or take the elevator) to a unique Manhattan getaway called The High Line. Today, the Whitney Museum of American Art is in the process of planning a six-story, Renzo Piano-designed satellite museum that will one day stand at this location. Elevated trains once ran here, transporting goods from the piers, warehouses, and the Meatpacking District to vendors across America.

32. Today, the High Line a landscaped promenade. Relax along the Hudson River to the west, strolling above the traffic, where you can observe historic Chelsea to the east.

View of the General Theological Seminary in Chelsea from the High Line

Lafayette Street, 1912

ASTOR PLACE

Astor Place takes its name from one of the most power families in New York history. This tour explores the area's artistic legacy—from the elegant townhouses straight out of Henry James' *Washington Square* to the studios of the Ashcan School and today's Public Theater.

Tour Time: about 1.5 hours
This Tour Contains Chapters: 5, 6, 10, 16

START:
Washington Square

SUBWAYS:
Ⓑ Ⓓ Ⓕ Ⓜ or Ⓐ Ⓒ Ⓔ
to West 4th Street
Ⓝ Ⓡ to 8th Street/NYU
❻ to Astor Place

END:
Astor Library

SUBWAYS:
Ⓝ Ⓡ at 8th Street/NYU
❻ at Astor Place

1. Start at the fountain in Washington Square. Before plumbing was installed under Greenwich Village streets, this was the site of the communal well where Village residents pumped their water.

2. In New York's earliest years, this park was a potter's field, a mass burial ground for indigent New Yorkers and those who died of cholera. There are thousands of unmarked graves beneath these paving stones in Washington Square.

3. The marble arch featuring General George Washington was designed by renowned architect Stanford White and built in 1892; it marks the beginning of Fifth Avenue.

4. All along the northern end of the park, Washington Square North is lined with some of the earliest luxury residences in America. Although they originally lacked indoor plumbing, these townhouses were built as homes for some of New York's wealthiest families. Henry James' famous novel *Washington Square* imagines life in these elegant homes; it's the source material for both the award-winning play and movie *The Heiress*. Henry James lived and worked from One Washington Square North; novelist Edith Wharton lived at No. 7. Today, most of these buildings are used as offices for New York University.

5. At the northwest corner of the park, turn right and cross Washington Square North, heading uptown on MacDougal Street.

6. Halfway up the block on the right (east) side, you'll find MacDougal Alley. These small buildings once housed the carriages owned by the residents of the townhouses on Washington Square North. Decades later, they gained fame when Gertrude Vanderbilt Whitney and other artists gentrified these empty buildings into art studios, which art critics dubbed "the Ashcan School." Some of the artists who joined Mrs. Whitney included: Robert Henri, George Bellows, William Glackens, George Luks, Everett Shinn, and John Sloan. Attracted by the art scene, Jackson Pollock moved into 9 MacDougal Alley in 1949.

7. Continue walking north on MacDougal Street, then turn right onto Eighth Street and walk east. You'll pass 8 West 8th Street, a building acquired by Gertrude Vanderbilt Whitney and the Ashcan artists as a place to display their art. It's the original site of the Whitney Museum of American Art.

8. Cross Fifth Avenue at the corner of Eighth Street and turn right (south) past the One Fifth Avenue apartment house. Halfway down the block you'll discover the Washington Mews, two rows of carriages houses formerly owned by the residents on Washington Square. Notice the original Belgian blocks that pave this street. All of Greenwich Village was once paved with these brick-shaped stones.

9. Walk all the way through the Washington Mews and you'll emerge on the campus of New York University, the largest private educational institution in the United States, and one of the largest owners of real estate in New York City. Turn right, heading south toward Washington Square East.

10. At the corner of Washington Place, turn left and walk further east, through the New York University campus, to the corner of Greene Street.

11. The Triangle Shirtwaist Company once stood at this northeast corner. In 1911, a spark from a primitive

electric sewing machine ignited the former building. Women laborers, locked in the building while working, jumped from the windows to their deaths as the fire raged out of control. The tragic scene led to new fire-safety laws, workers rights, and the creation of the International Ladies' Garment Workers' Union.

12. Continue walking east on Washington Place; then turn left on Broadway, heading uptown. These Broadway buildings were the sites of many garment-related industries, with a showroom on the ground floor and sweatshops upstairs. Today, some of these buildings have been converted into residential lofts, while others are still used for offices and light manufacturing.

13. On Broadway between 10th and 11th streets, you'll find Grace Church, the first construction project by architect James Renwick, who gained greater fame as the architect for Saint Patrick's Cathedral. Prior to this church's construction, the site was a grove of trees maintained by owner Hendrick Brevoort, who guarded the site with a live bear.

14. Turn right on 10th Street to walk further east. At Lafayette Street, turn right and walk down to Astor Place. For most of the 20th century, this neighborhood was home to people of Eastern-European ancestry.

15. The Cooper Union (the brown building on Astor Place) is one of America's oldest and most prestigious colleges for art, architecture and engineering. Tuition is free and competition for acceptance is fierce, with less than five percent of applicants awarded acceptance. Abraham Lincoln debated Stephen Douglas in the Great Hall at Cooper Union, which led to his nomination for president. Subsequent presidents to speak in the Great Hall include Ulysses Grant, William Taft, Theodore Roosevelt, Woodrow Wilson, Bill Clinton, and Barack Obama.

16. Cross Third Avenue as you continue walking east. Astor Place and Cooper Square become St. Mark's Place, famous in the 1960s as the place for New York's hippie community to congregate. Gentrification has turned this into a multi-cultural neighborhood today, with many NYU students as residents as well.

17. Continue to the end of the block, then turn right onto Second Avenue, walk one block south, then turn right again, onto 7th Street.

18. At 15 East 7th Street, you'll find McSorley's Old Ale House, the last of New York's "men only" pubs, until it was "liberated" by Gloria Steinem, an action successfully defended in court by the National Organization for Women in 1970. Today, McSorley's welcomes men and women patrons.

19. Walking west, you'll pass Surma, a fascinating Ukrainian shop that has imported and sold handmade Eastern-European artifacts since the early twentieth century.

20. Continuing to the west, you'll pass the modern School of Architecture at the Cooper Union. The triangular park between the old and new buildings at Cooper Union was the site of riots protesting the government's Civil War draft.

21. Continue west, crossing Cooper Square Park, then turn right on Fourth Avenue, heading again toward Astor Place. At the corner, turn left (west) and walk to Lafayette Street, then turn left again to walk down Lafayette Street.

22. Observe the buildings across Lafayette Street. The building at 436-440 Lafayette Street has a facade completely constructed of cast-iron. Others nearby have large sections of cast-iron set into the bricks. This precedent-setting process enabled builders to construct New York's large buildings more rapidly, and at a lower cost than assembling

bricks and mortar. The process would later morph into construction with large panels of glass and steel, today's famed New York City skyscrapers.

23. Further down the block, notice the buildings with tall Greek columns. Built by John Jacob Astor as a much larger row of attached, opulent one-family townhouses, including one for oldest son William B. Astor and family, identical buildings once occupied most of the block, known as The Colonnade. Over the decades many of these townhouses were demolished; the remaining facades are now local landmarks, a reminder of what is lost when neighborhoods evolve through new construction.

24. Across the street stands the former home of the Astor Library, built by John Jacob Astor to house his book collection. (It was later merged with books from James Lenox and Samuel Tilden to become the New York Public Library at Fifth Avenue and 42nd Street.) Before Astor constructed this redbrick library, this was the site of the eighteen hundred-seat Astor Place Opera House, which was destroyed when "patriotic" Americans protested the appearance of a British performer soon after the War of 1812. Today the Astor Library has been reconfigured into The Public Theater. Some of Broadway's greatest successes began in this building, including the original productions of *Hair* and *A Chorus Line*, a terrific example of how old construction can adapt to accommodate modern times.

The Colonnade, 1831

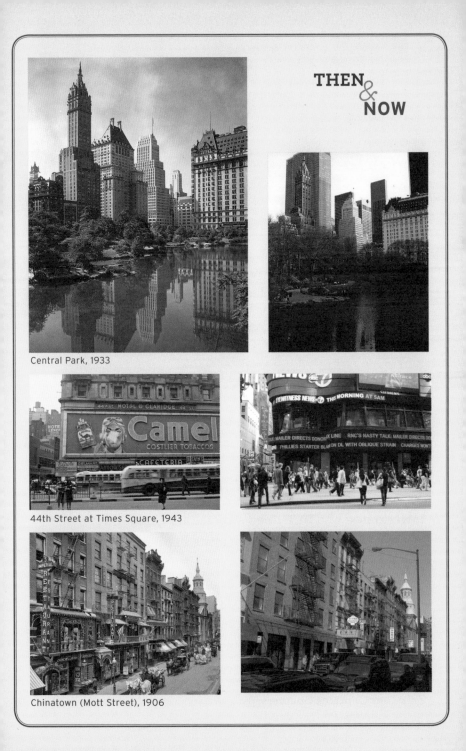

THEN & NOW

Central Park, 1933

44th Street at Times Square, 1943

Chinatown (Mott Street), 1906

Gramercy Park, 1935

GRAMERCY PARK

Gramercy Park is the only private park in Manhattan. Though only key-holders may enter, the charming townhouses and tree-lined streets that surround it make up one of the most beautiful sights in Manhattan.

Tour Time: about 1.5 hours
This Tour Contains Chapters: 8, 14, 15

START:
Madison Square Park

SUBWAYS:
Ⓡ to 23rd Street
❻ to 23rd Street
Ⓕ Ⓜ to 23rd Street

END:
Union Square

SUBWAYS:
Ⓛ or Ⓝ Ⓠ Ⓡ or ❹ ❺ ❻
at Union Square

1. Broadway intersects Fifth Avenue at 23rd Street, creating an unusual triangle where one of the world's first skyscrapers, the Flatiron Building, was constructed. New Yorkers feared that it would be toppled by the wind, but its unseen superstructure of steel beneath the stone facade proved the durability of high-rise architecture instead.

2. The Flatiron's unusual shape caused winds to swirl toward Madison Square Park, frequently causing ladies' skirts to rise. Awaiting the glimpse of an ankle, young men often lined 23rd Street at Madison Square Park until Police Officers gave them the "23-skidoo."

3. This location is also notable for the office buildings facing into Madison Square Park. Renowned architect Stanford White maintained his office here.

4. On Broadway, walk south (downtown) past the Flatiron Building (also known as 175 Fifth Avenue). The buildings from 14th Street to 23rd Street were known as Ladies' Mile for the fine fashions and millinery shops located here. These streets were once a fashion parade.

5. The cast-iron building at the corner of Broadway and 20th Street (909 Broadway) is the former location of the Lord & Taylor department store. Turn left at this corner, heading east. (East 20th Street is also labeled Theodore Roosevelt Way.)

6. The brownstone at 28 East 20th Street was the childhood home of President Theodore Roosevelt,

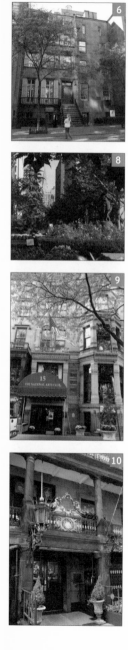

who was born in 1858 and lived here for the first fifteen years of his life. Maintained by the National Parks Service, this National Historic Landmark is open for tours Tuesday through Saturday.

7. Continue walking east. Upon crossing Park Avenue South, you'll enter the Gramercy Park Historic District, named for the landscaped park directly ahead.

8. Gramercy Park is New York's only private park, just two blocks wide and one block long. Residents in the buildings surrounding the park are its sole key-holders, adding extra value to these exclusive addresses. Continue to walk east along this southern perimeter of the private park.

9. On the right, you'll discover the National Arts Club, built by Samuel Tilden (later a presidential candidate) and remodeled into a club by Calvert Vaux, the designer of Central Park. (The interiors of the club can be seen in Martin Scorsese's film *The Age of Innocence* starring Daniel Day-Lewis and Winona Ryder.) Past members have included artists Frederick Remington and Robert Henri, and presidents Theodore Roosevelt and Woodrow Wilson.

10. Next door at 16 Gramercy Park South is the Players Club, another National Historic Landmark; its interior is only open to club members. Founded by Edwin Booth and Mark Twain, among others, it is the foremost gathering place for America's stage actors. Some current members include: Edie Falco, Ethan Hawke, Timothy Hutton, Al Pacino, Carol Burnett, Mary Tyler Moore; the list goes on.

11. Turn to the left (north) to view Gramercy Park East. The building at the corner, 34 Gramercy Park is the first cooperative apartment building in New York. (Unlike today's condominiums, co-op owners buy shares in the building, much like joining a country club. Technically, selling a co-op apartment means selling those shares in the building corporation.)

James Cagney owned an apartment here, as did Margaret Hamilton, and John Carradine.

12. Walk to the corner of Gramercy Park East, then turn left (west) to stroll along Gramercy Park North. Near its center, notice the large gate where key-holding residents enter the park. Lexington Avenue begins here too, the street in the center that heads north. Julia Roberts, Victor Herbert, John Steinbeck, Thomas Edison, John Barrymore and Stanford White are just some of the many acclaimed individuals past and present who owned a key to this private park.

13. At the corner of the park, turn left (south) to view Gramercy Park West.

14. The building at 3 Gramercy Park West was the final home for actor John Garfield, starring in a revival of *Golden Boy* on Broadway when he died. No. 4 Gramercy Park was the home of James Harper, publisher of *Harper's Magazine*, which featured stories by local authors such as Herman Melville, Mark Twain, and Horace Greeley. (His publishing company Harper & Row, today's Harper-Collins, has given us works by Tom Wolfe and Jonathan Franzen among many others.) Harper was elected Mayor of New York in 1844.

15. Turn left (east) at the corner of Gramercy Park South, and stroll past the Players Club toward the intersecting street near the center of the park.

16. That intersecting street is Irving Place, named for renowned New York writer Washington Irving. Turn right (south) to stroll down Irving Place.

17. At the corner of Irving Place and East 18th Street, you'll find Pete's Tavern, one of the oldest continuously functioning bars in Manhattan, established in 1864. It was immortalized by writer and frequent patron O. Henry (a resident at 55 Irving Place), who drank himself to death by cirrhosis of the liver in the days before Prohibition.

18. For an architectural treat, turn left (east) on 18th Street. While most Manhattan townhouses feature tall stoops with many stairs (like those along Gramercy Park West), the entrances to these landmark townhouses feature an "English basement," just a few steps up to the front door and a few steps down for the servant's entrance below. These are some of the oldest houses still standing in New York.

19. Turn around and return to Irving Place, crossing to the west side of the street, then turn left (south) to continue the downtown walk.

20. At the corner of 17th Street, the building at 49 Irving Place (also known as 122 East 17th Street) was the home of Washington Irving, author of *The Legend of Sleepy Hollow* among other titles; it was Irving who coined the term "Gotham" to refer to New York City. He also served as the first chairman of the Astor Library.

21. Turn right to walk west on 17th Street. Directly ahead you'll see Union Square, the site of the first Labor Day celebration on September 5, 1882. It's been a center of political activism ever since: the place where Emma Goldman and generations of rabble-rousers have led protests and marches in their fight for human rights.

Manhattan looking south on Turtle Bay and Tudor City, 1931

TURTLE BAY

Once a marshy farmland, Turtle Bay has become home to movie stars and ambassadors alike. This tour starts in the international territory of the United Nations Headquarters, and ends at Riverview Terrace, one of Manhattan's most exclusive addresses.

Tour Time: about 2.5 hours
This Tour Contains Chapters: 9, 25

START:
United Nations

END:
Sutton Square

SUBWAYS:
4 **5** **6** or **7**
to Grand Central-42nd Street

SUBWAYS:
4 **5** **6** at 59th Street
N **R** **Q** at 59th Street

1. From the United Nations, cross First Avenue to its western side.

2. Walk north up First Avenue following the direction of the traffic to 47th Street. On the right, on First Avenue spanning 47th to 48th streets is Trump World Tower, currently the tallest residential building in Manhattan.

3. Walk west on 47th Street, also known as Dag Hammarskjold Plaza, the site of many demonstrations for human rights.

4. At Second Avenue, turn right. Walk north (uptown) one block. Take a left on 48th Street.

5. These are the historic Turtle Bay Gardens townhouses, all linked by an elegant common garden in back. Author E.B. White lived at 229 East 48th Street while writing *Charlotte's Web*. Walk around this block by heading west, then north on Third Avenue; then view the other side of the complex from 49th Street, heading back to the east. Residents of these townhouses have included Katharine Hepburn (244 East 49th Street), Oscar-winning writer/director Garson Kanin with his actress wife Ruth Gordon (242 East 49th Street) composer Stephen Sondheim, and *Time* magazine publisher Henry Luce (234 East 49th Street).

6. Continue walking west on 49th Street to First Avenue.

7. Across First Avenue is UN Plaza, mixed-use condominium apartments. The building at 780 UN Plaza was once home to Johnny Carson and Truman Capote, among others.

8. Cross First Avenue at 49th Street; then follow the upper ramp onto Mitchell Place. Walk one block further east toward the East River and Beekman Place.

9. At the corner, you'll face One Beekman Place, the former home of John D. Rockefeller III. More notoriously, it was also the home to Mame Dennis, known as Auntie Mame in the famous book by her nephew, author Patrick Dennis, and in vivid incarnations on stage and in film. Mame's penthouse was later owned by the equally flamboyant Huntington Hartford, heir to a grocery-store fortune.

10. Continue to walk north to East 50th Street.

11. The redbrick building at the corner of 50th Street (17 Beekman Place) was the one-family home of composer Irving Berlin, who lived in the house for the final four decades of his life. It's now the Luxembourg Consulate.

12. Turn left and stroll across and back on 50th Street. These elegant townhouses have been the homes to Oscar-nominee Dame Judith Anderson (414 East 50th Street), Oscar-nominee Julie Harris (415 East 50th Street), and architect Max Abramowitz (419 East 50th Street), whose prominent works include the headquarters for the United Nations and Avery Fisher Hall at Lincoln Center.

13. Return to Beekman Place and observe the row of townhouses along its eastern side. While most buildings are now consulates for foreign governments, these former one-family residences have been the homes of architect Paul Rudolph (23 Beekman Place), award-winning author William Shirer (25-27 Beekman Place), Broadway producer Billy Rose (29 Beekman Place), and Ashraf Pahlavi, the sister of the Shah of Iran (33 Beekman Place). Perhaps most notably, Aristotle Onassis purchased the house at the corner of 51st Street (39 Beekman Place) as a gift for his new bride Jacqueline Kennedy Onassis. The paparazzi promptly set up

a full-time vigil outside the house. Observing the lack of privacy, the Onassises never moved in.

14. At the corner of 51st Street, turn right and walk down the stairs and across the footbridge that leads to the East River. At the end of the bridge (or from the park below), you'll see grand apartment houses. Before these buildings were erected, the was a neighborhood in decline, the subject of the play and movie *Dead End* starring Humphrey Bogart and introducing The Dead End Kids, who went on to appear in a succession of films as the Bowery Boys.

15. On the other side of the East River is Roosevelt Island, a large complex of apartments accessible from Manhattan by a tram suspended on cables over the East River. Beyond it, the neon Silvercup sign advertises the site of a former commercial bakery that now serves as the Silvercup Studios, used for many film and television productions.

16. Facing downtown, you'll see a terrific view of the United Nations and the Williamsburg Bridge.

17. Return to Beekman Place; then walk west toward First Avenue. Stroll up First Avenue; then turn right onto 52nd Street. Note the Dead End sign. This was once the squalid home of the real-life Dead End Kids portrayed in films and on Broadway.

18. Two important buildings overlook the water. River House at 435 East 52nd Street has been the home to former Secretary of State Henry Kissinger, stage and film director Joshua Logan, *Time* magazine publisher Henry Luce and his playwright wife Clare Booth Luce; also Marshall Field, Cornelius Vanderbilt Whitney, and Angier Biddle Duke.

19. Across the street, 450 East 52nd Street was the home of singer Bobby Short, British playwright and actor Noël Coward, and Broadway's leading lady Mary Martin. Most notably, Greta Garbo, the film star who "wanted to be alone," found her solace here for the last half of her life.

20. Return to First Avenue and walk up to 54th Street, then turn right.

21. Note the large condominium halfway down the block, River Tower. One of its very first residents was the Iron Butterfly Imelda Marcos, wife of the deposed Philippine dictator, who reportedly arrived with over four hundred pairs of shoes.

22. Continue east to the corner of Sutton Place South; then turn left, heading uptown on Sutton Place South. The building at 36 Sutton Place South (between 55th and 56th streets) was the home of Joan Crawford during the 1950s.

23. Sutton Place is one of New York's most exclusive addresses. Liza Minnelli lives around the corner on East 57th Street, and actress Helen Hayes, the record-setting performer who won an Oscar, a Grammy, an Emmy and a Tony Award, made her home at 444 East 57th Street. Stage and film star Lillian Fish called 430 East 57th Street home for decades. Perhaps most notably, Marilyn Monroe and Arthur Miller lived on the 13th floor of 444 East 57th Street.

24. Feelin' groovy? Walk East to the small park overlooking the river, where you'll have a great photo op of the 59th Street Bridge (more formally: the Queensboro Bridge) made famous by Simon and Garfunkel in their "59th Street Bridge Song." If you time it right, you might even catch a photo of the Roosevelt Island tram in mid-air.

25. Walk up Sutton Place toward 58th Street. This row of townhouses along the east side has been owned by a number of illustrious residents. One Sutton Place has been home to oil baron J. Paul Getty, and later to H.J. Heinz II of Heinz Ketchup fame and former father-in-law of Teresa Heinz Kerry. Two Sutton Place was the home of entertainer George Jessel, and later, playwright William Saroyan.

26. At 58th Street, notice that the name changes to Sutton Square. Walk east toward the river and you'll find one of New York most private cul-de-sacs, called Riverview Terrace.

Park Avenue north from 50th Street

MIDTOWN

Midtown Manhattan is home to many of the great
modern icons of New York City, including the New York
Public Library, Rockefeller Center, and the Chrysler
Building. A stroll through the area reveals traces of the
many entrepreneurs who have shaped Manhattan, from
Commodore Vanderbilt to Donald Trump.

Tour Time: about 2 hours
This Tour Contains Chapters: 11, 12, 19, 25

START:
Grand Central Terminal

SUBWAYS:
④ ⑤ ⑥ or ⑤

to Grand Central-42nd Street

END:
Saint Bartholomew's Church

SUBWAYS:
⑥ at 51st Street

1. Start in Grand Central Terminal, at the information desk marked by an opulent brass clock; its faces are precious opal. Cornelius Vanderbilt purchased the land here in 1869 for use as a train depot and rail yard. The current Beaux-Arts building—designed by two firms, Warren and Wetmore, and Reed and Stem—opened in 1913. To this day it is one of the world's busiest train stations, serving over 750,000 passengers a day.

2. Look up inside the Grand Concourse. The ceiling is painted with a mural of the zodiac designed by French artist Paul Helleu. If the vision of the sky looks unfamiliar, that's because it's painted backwards. The mural was restored as part of a program that began in 1996.

3. Exit the station via the corner of 42nd Street and Lexington Avenue exit.

4. The Chrysler Building is located directly across the street. The Art Deco building was completed in 1930, and was then the tallest building in the world for just eleven months, until the completion of the Empire State Building.

5. Turn right (west) on 42nd Street. Here you will pass the Grand Hyatt New York, originally called the Commodore Hotel when it was built in 1919. Sixty years later, Donald Trump purchased the dilapidated property for a mere $10 million. Here "The Donald" created his signature look of mirrored finishes and polished stainless steel. The hotel was a key moment in the revitalization of Midtown, and in establishing Trump as a major force in New York real estate.

6. Continue walking west on 42nd Street, past Grand Central Terminal on your right.

7. Continue walking west until you reach Fifth Avenue. Here, on your left (south), you will see the New York Public Library, designed by Carrère and Hastings, a little-known firm at the time. The cornerstone was laid in 1902 and construction was completed in 1911. The project cost $9 million (the equivalent of well over $200 million today).

8. In front of the library sit two famous lions—originally called Leo Astor and Leo Lenox after the library's founders. They gained the more popular nicknames Patience and Fortitude from Mayor Fiorello La Guardia during the Great Depression. Facing the library, Patience is on your left (south) and Fortitude is to the right (north).

9. This was once home to the Croton Reservoir, which stored drinking water from the Croton River in Westchester. The foundation of the Reservoir can still be seen in the Library's South Court.

10. Head north on Fifth Avenue, toward 44th Street. Sherry's Hotel moved here in 1898, to a building designed by McKim, Mead & White; spot it by the landmark clock located outside. The hotel was a symbol of Gilded Age extravagance—once hosting a dinner where guests dined on horseback—until Prohibition shut it down in 1919.

11. One block up Fifth Avenue, at 45th Street, you will see the landmark Fred F. French building, named after the founder of Tudor City. Notice its gold embellishments and decorative motifs inspired by the Hanging Gardens of Babylon.

12. As you continue walking north on Fifth Avenue glance down 47th Street. This is known as the Diamond District. Over 90 percent of diamonds that enter the United States come through New York, and most of those stop here.

13. At 50th Street you will reach Rockefeller Center on your left. One of the most beautiful and well-known landmarks in Manhattan, this Art Deco building complex contains Radio City Music Hall, the International Building, as well as shops and dining in the underground Concourse. The plaza is filled with artwork and ornamentation, including Isamu Noguchi's *News*, a stainless steel bas-relief over the entrance of the Associated Press Building.

14. The centerpiece of Rockefeller Center is the GE Building, the home to NBC Studios. Take a moment to view the lobby at "30 Rock", featuring the mural *American Progress*, painted by Jose Maria Sert. The mural replaced a controversial work by famed Mexican muralist Diego Rivera, deemed unacceptable by Nelson Rockefeller for its depiction of Vladimir Lenin.

15. Exit the GE Building and walk along the edge of the sunken plaza. Here you will see Paul Manship's famous gilded sculpture, *Prometheus*. In the winter the plaza is an ice-skating rink, in summer, an outdoor restaurant.

16. As you continue toward Fifth Avenue, take a moment to relax for a moment in the Channel Gardens. Named for the English Channel, the gardens separate La Maison Francaise and the British Empire Building. The space frequently hosts public art installations.

17. Saint Patrick's Cathedral is across the street. The Neo-Gothic structure is an oasis of calm in Midtown, and it's worth a trip inside. Designed by James Renwick, construction began in 1858 and lasted until 1878. The church is richly decorated, including stained-glass windows from Chartres, France and two altars designed by Tiffany & Co.

18. From the center aisle, turn and look out the doors—for a direct view of Lee Lawrie's famous *Atlas* statue.

19. Exit the cathedral and turn right, continuing north on Fifth Avenue, past the Versace store (647 Fifth Avenue). When the Italian luxury label opened here in 1996, this was the dilapidated former home of George W. Vanderbilt, the grandson of Cornelius Vanderbilt.

20. Turn left (west) down West 52nd Street. During Prohibition, this was known as "The Street" for its abundant speakeasies and jazz clubs. Today, you can still visit one of the most famous, the 21 Club—formerly known as Jack and Charlie's 21—at 21 West 52nd Street. Thirty-three jockey statues line its facade.

21. Travel east on 52nd Street, across Fifth Avenue. Make a right on Madison Avenue and continue south toward 50th Street. At the northeast corner of 50th Street and Madison Avenue stands the New York Palace Hotel.

22. Here, in 1882, Stanford White built the Villard Mansion, six private Italianate residences. When, in the 1970s, they were re-imagined as the Helmsley Palace Hotel, the Landmarks Preservation Committee prohibited demolition of the original structure. So Emery Roth and Sons designed a contemporary fifty-five-story tower above the structure. The hotel opened in 1980, and got a new taste of fame with its starring role on hit series *Gossip Girl*.

23. Continue along 50th Street to Park Avenue. Until about 1875, Park Avenue was dirty and undesirable, because of the trains that ran along the then-named Fourth Avenue.

24. On the eastern side of Park Avenue, across 50th Street from the Waldof=Astoria, you will approach Saint Bartholomew's Episcopal Church. Founded in 1835, it moved to this Byzantine-style building in 1918.

25. The bronze doors at Saint Bart's were designed by Stanford White in memory of Cornelius Vanderbilt II, the beloved grandson of Cornelius Vanderbilt.

The Dakota, 1884

UPPER WEST SIDE

The area of Manhattan west of Central Park is one of the most densely populated neighborhoods in the entire nation. It's also one of New York City's largest landmark districts, where rows of historic brownstones along tree-lined streets, built circa 1900, are mingled with magnificent apartment houses along Central Park West and the Hudson River.

Tour Time: about 1.5 hours
This Tour Contains Chapters: 13, 17

START:
The Ansonia

SUBWAY:
1 **2** **3** to 72nd Street

END:
Strawberry Fields

SUBWAY:
B **C** at 72nd Street

1. The Ansonia is one of the neighborhood's first apartment houses, located on Broadway between 73rd and 74th streets. It was built in 1899 as a hotel where guest checked in for months, or even years at a time. For many years its top floor tenants were Broadway impresario Florenz Ziegfeld and his wife Bille Burke (Glinda in *The Wizard of Oz*), though Ziegfeld kept another apartment for ex-wife Anna Held on the floor below plus a tenth-floor apartment for his paramour Lillian Lorraine! Other residents included Enrico Caruso, Arturo Toscanini, Igor Stravinsky, and opera star Ezio Pinza. Decades later, its ground floor gained even greater notoriety as The Continental Baths, the gay bathhouse that launched the career of Bette Midler.

2. Take a right onto 74th Street, heading east toward Central Park.

3. While walking on 74th Street, cross Amsterdam Avenue and observe the historic brownstones in this landmark neighborhood. Though many alterations have occurred over the decades (many stoops were removed), these buildings were once erected as single-family dwellings. Today, most have been divided into several apartments.

4. On Columbus Avenue, turn left (north). It's an important shopping street for residents of this neighborhood, with many boutiques and one-of-a-kind restaurants.

5. Continue walking uptown, past the William J. O'Shea Jr. High School. At the corner of 77th Street and Columbus Avenue, turn right.

6. Walk east, on 77th Street toward Central Park. On the left, you'll pass the American Museum of Natural History, famous for its dinosaur skeleton exhibits, also home to the equally astounding Hayden Planetarium.

7. On the right, you'll view some important apartment houses with magnificent views over Central Park. Renowned artist Helen Frankenthaler lived and worked here for years.

8. Continue walking toward Central Park. At the corner (170 Central Park West) is the New-York Historical Society, a museum of New York's history, which features a reference library and important archive collection.

9. Cross the street to walk along the sidewalk beside Central Park.

10. This is an ideal vantage point for viewing the magnificent apartment houses that line Central Park West in both directions, built before World War II, including several by eminent architect Emery Roth. Almost all are co-ops, where current residents decide to accept or reject potential new neighbors. With that kind of security, these buildings are home to many celebrities. Some residents past and present include: Dustin Hoffman, Katie Couric, Liz Smith, Mary Tyler Moore, Steve Jobs, Bono, and Madonna; the list goes on and on.

11. Then turn and head downtown (south). The building directly ahead, between 73rd and 72nd streets is The Dakota. Built in 1884, it was first building to be erected in this neighborhood, when Central Park was actually an undesirable collection of shanties built by squatters. The Dakota is famous as the first luxury apartment house in America. The building has been home to a seemingly endless list of celebrities that has included Boris Karloff, Leonard Bernstein, Lauren Bacall, Rudolf Nureyev, Roberta

Flack. Rosemary Clooney, Jason Robards, José Fer-
rer, and many more. It is also remembered as the sad
place where John Lennon was assassinated by Mark
David Chapman as he returned home with Yoko Ono
from the Record Plant Studio on December 8, 1980.

12. At the corner of 72nd Street, turn left
    (east) and enter Central Park.

13. Walk straight ahead, bearing to the left where
    you'll see a blacktop path and sign labeled
    Strawberry Fields. Follow this path as it curves
    to the right in the shady park. You'll soon en-
    counter a memorial to the late John Lennon,
    a place to relax or to explore Central Park.

Harlem, 1944

HARLEM

Harlem is a district that is comprised of several neighborhoods. Here are three areas of historic interest that can be explored separately on foot: Astor Row, Strivers' Row, and Sugar Hill.

Tour Time: about 1 hour each
This Tour Contains Chapters: 20

ASTOR ROW

START:
Fifth Avenue at 130th Street

END:
The Apollo Theater

SUBWAYS:
2 **3** to 125th Street
4 **5** **6** to 125th Street

SUBWAYS:
2 **3** at 125th Street
4 **5** **6** at 125th Street

Much of today's Harlem was purchased as undeveloped land by John Jacob Astor. His grandson William Backhouse Astor developed the rare block of townhouses located between Fifth Avenue and Lenox Avenue on 130th Street, now known as Astor Row, protected as a New York City landmark for their rare wooden porches and front yards.

1. At Fifth Avenue walk west on 130th Street, observing Astor Row. At the corner of Lenox Avenue, turn left (south) to walk down Lenox Avenue.

2. You'll pass Sylvia's Restaurant (between 126th and 127th streets), a local landmark, serving soul food to Harlem residents and famous visitors since 1962. Every politician visiting Harlem, from Nelson Mandela to Bill Clinton, has dined at Sylvia's Restaurant of Harlem.

3. Continue walking south on Lenox Avenue (also known as Malcolm X Boulevard) to the corner of 125th Street; then turn left (east).

4. Although 125th Street is often called the "Main Street" of Harlem, it's alternate name is actually Martin Luther King, Jr. Boulevard.

5. The offices of President Bill Clinton are located at 55 West 125th Street, in the middle of the block between Lenox Avenue and Fifth Avenue.

6. Remain on 125th Street by turning around and walking to the west.

7. Cross Lenox Avenue and Seventh Avenue (also known as Adam Clayton Powell, Jr. Boulevard). Directly ahead at 253 West 125th Street, you'll see the Apollo Theater, a National Historic Landmark.

8. Built in 1913, the Apollo Theater has been refurbished several times and is now owned by the State of New York. Originally a burlesque theater, in 1934 the Apollo introduced its famous Amateur Night contests that launched the careers of countless performers. That year, seventeen-year-old Ella Fitzgerald won $25 as an Apollo amateur; her prolific career and an Apollo tradition were born. Some other famous performers (though not amateurs) at the Apollo include: Billie Holliday, Aretha Franklin, James Brown, Stevie Wonder, Marvin Gaye, Luther Vandross, Diana Ross, the Jackson 5, and many more. The lobby and gift shop are open to visitors during business hours.

STRIVERS' ROW

START:
Abyssinian Baptist Church

END:
Strivers' Row

SUBWAYS:
Ⓑ Ⓒ to 135 Street
② ③ to 135th Street

SUBWAY:
② ③ at 135th Street

Born in 1865, at the end of the Civil War, Adam Clayton Powell, Sr. was the son of an African-Cherokee slave woman and a white slave owner. It was his stepfather, a former slave, who introduced a young Powell to the Bible. He studied theology at the Yale Divinity School and became pastor of the Abyssinian Baptist Church in Harlem in 1908. As the black population of Harlem grew exponentially, Reverend Powell was its dynamic leader, uniting the community into one of the largest Protestant congregations anywhere in America. He was an early leader in the National Urban League and the NAACP, and a charismatic lecturer.

In 1937, his son Adam Clayton Powell Jr. succeeded him as pastor of the Abyssinian Baptist Church, after attending nearby City College and Columbia University. The younger Powell used the strength of Harlem's large population to crusade for jobs and housing. He forced the utility companies to hire black employees, and organized a bus boycott until 200 black workers were hired by the transit authority. Adam Clayton Powell Jr. was the first black man to be elected to the New York City Council in 1941, and just three years later he was elected to the U.S. House of Representatives as the delegate from Harlem, the first black Congressman from New York.

1. Start at Lenox Avenue (Malcolm X Boulevard) and 138th Street and walk west toward Adam Clayton Powell Jr. Boulevard. The Abyssinian Baptist Church is in the middle of the block. (Everyone is welcome for Sunday services, but the place is always packed, so plan to arrive very early.)

2. Cross 138th Street at the corner of Adam Clayton Powell Jr. Boulevard to visit one of Harlem's most important blocks, known as Strivers' Row. In Harlem's heyday, these townhouses were the homes for songwriters Eubie Blake and Noble Sissle, "father of the blues" W.C. Handy, comedian Stepin Fetchit, singer-dancer Bill "Bojangles" Robinson, and Adam Clayton Powell, Jr. Continue walking west along Strivers' Row.

3. At the corner of Frederick Douglass Boulevard, turn right (north). Halfway up the block you will see the entrance to the alley where owners of Striver's Row townhouses stabled their horses. Today they are garages, a rare commodity anywhere in Manhattan.

4. Continue walking north on Frederick Douglass Boulevard. At the corner of 139th Street, turn right (east) to observe the other side of Strivers' Row. The townhouses on the north side of 139th Street were all designed and decorated by famed architect Stanford White.

SUGAR HILL

START:
Convent Avenue at 145th Street

END:
Convent Avenue at 155th Street

SUBWAYS:
① to 145th Street
Ⓐ Ⓒ or Ⓑ Ⓓ to 145th Street

SUBWAYS:
Ⓒ to 155th Street
Ⓑ Ⓓ to 155th Street

Sugar Hill is possibly the most beautiful neighborhood in Harlem. While most of the hills and valleys throughout Manhattan were leveled over a century ago, this hill remained intact, with elegant townhouses built on its high ground.

Located a few blocks north of City College of New York (CCNY), in an area of Harlem called Hamilton Heights, the Sugar Hill Historic District officially extends from 145th to 155th streets, bounded by Edgecomb Avenue on the east and Amsterdam Avenue on the west.

The neighborhood got its name in the 1920s when it was when it was a symbol of the "sweet life" available to upscale African-Americans in Harlem. It was declared both a Historic District by the New York City Landmarks Preservation Commission in 2000, and a National Registered Historic Place.

1. Convent Avenue is the center boulevard of the landmark district. To view the architecture of this historic place, start at Convent Avenue at 145th Street.

2. Head north toward 155th Street, winding your way through the attractive tree-lined streets both to the east and west of Convent Avenue.

3. Famous residents here have included Chief Justice Thurgood Marshall, bandleader Duke Ellington and composer Billy Strayhorn.

4. End your tour at 155th Street, the neighborhood's northern boundary.

TOWNHOUSE STYLE

Labels like Greek Revival, Anglo-Italianate, and Federal, among other terms, define architectural variances in New York's historical real estate. Listed chronologically, these townhouse styles illustrate a brief history of residential construction in New York.

COLONIAL / GEORGIAN

ERA: Prior to the Revolutionary War

DISTINGUISHING TRAITS: wooden exterior, pointed roof

HISTORY: The oldest houses in New York are also its most rare. Fewer than ten wooden houses remain on Manhattan island. Built before the grid was devised for Manhattan's streets, wooden houses were erected on gently rolling farmland. Situated in erratic locations that didn't conform to the visions of city planners, most were demolished. Although the interiors of these last Colonial houses have been drastically renovated to accommodate modern plumbing and storage, their exteriors are landmarks as they are the oldest constructions still standing in urban America.

EARLY FEDERAL

ERA: 1780–1810

DISTINGUISHING TRAITS: Exterior red brick walls, usually three stories tall, with pointed roofs to accommodate the run-off from the severe weather the British builders anticipated. Stabilized by an extra-strong brick pattern known as Flemish Bond, each room has a fireplace except on the top floor, where a short chimney risked downdrafts that might blow burning embers onto the wooden floors.

HISTORY: With low ceilings and no ornamentation, these were not popular houses to restore since few New Yorkers would choose to live the spartan life of the city's early residents.

BEST SEEN IN: the landmark district west of Sixth Avenue, below Houston Street (Charlton Street, King Street, Vandam Street). Look for the pointed roofs.

LATE FEDERAL

ERA: 1810–1830s

DISTINGUISHING TRAITS: Flat roofs, exterior walls constructed of bricks, with wooden beams set within them, spanning the full width of the house. The house has no "bearing walls" except the actual brick exterior itself.

HISTORY: Since their architects were schooled in England, Federal houses draw heavily from concepts employed in England, including the "English basement." From the sidewalk, a short stoop leads up to the parlor floor, while a short stair downwards provides the service entrance to the ground floor kitchen. There is no cellar below. As decades rolled by, it became apparent that New York was not a land of daily rain. Progressing to a flat roof, owners gained desperately needed space on the top floor. To display their newfound prosperity, Federal houses display the first traces of ornamentation, especially around the single front door, with slender pillars, leaded sidelight windows, and lead-glass transoms.

BEST SEEN IN: Greenwich Village, especially west of Bleecker Street; Perry Street, Bank Street, Jane Street and environs. Easily identified by the brick facades.

GREEK REVIVAL

ERA: 1820 to 1840

DISTINGUISHING TRAITS: Similar to a Federal townhouse, built of brick, but with Ionic or Doric columns flanking the single front door, as well as a taller, more imposing stoop. While these houses feature a separate service entrance under the stoop, they also include a full height cellar below grade.

HISTORY: As New York residents prospered, that success was displayed in the heights of their houses and ceilings. The exterior ornamentation provides a hint of the details installed within: elaborate doors of mahogany or rosewood separate the two main parlor rooms, while moldings feature a Greek key or Dentil pattern above. Wainscoting or chair rails wrap around the room, while floors are often planks one-foot wide and one inch thick. Still, city life was far from genteel. Those charming gardens behind today's townhouses had a brutally practical domestic application for the original residents. With the kitchen always situated on the ground floor rear, the yard beyond the kitchen door was the place where pigs were butchered and carpets beaten. Since the city government didn't begin to install plumbing under the streets until the 1830s, it was the site of the cistern and the outhouse.

BEST SEEN IN: Greenwich Village, along the north side of Washington Square, and Chelsea's Cushman Row, 406-418 West 20th Street.

GOTHIC REVIVAL

ERA: 1830s to 1850s

DISTINGUISHING TRAITS: The iconic brownstone arrives. Built of bricks like a Greek Revival townhouse, but faced with a layer of brownstone. Hard Greek symmetry is exchanged for graceful arches.

HISTORY: A romantic movement was sweeping through art and literature. As Henry David Thoreau, the Hudson River School artists, James Fenimore Cooper, and Washington Irving glorified nature, architects responded by applying natural brownstone to the facades, learning to work in a medium that would soon soar in demand. Ornamental features like repeating floral patterns and curves were put to more successful use on Trinity Church (on Broadway at Wall Street, completed in 1846) than in local residences.

BEST SEEN IN: Brooklyn Heights: Willow Street, State Street, Pierrepont Street, and environs. Also visible in some of Manhattan's finest churches, including Saint Patrick's Cathedral and Grace Church.

THE BROWNSTONE ERA

By 1850, New York was the most prosperous city in America. Its population tripled over thirty years, driving a nonstop building boom. Houses got smaller but were built more rapidly, with interior decorations ordered from architectural catalogs. "Gingerbread" ornamentation became the order of the day, as self-made aristocrats flaunted their success in pliable brownstone carvings. Some of those styles include:

ITALIANATE
ERA: 1850 to 1880
DISTINGUISHING TRAITS: Rusticated or rough-hewn brownstone at the bottom, smooth brownstone above. Corinthian columns at the double front door, garlands molded into the cornices. Marble mantels in every room.
HISTORY: Monumental in style, patterned after the Italian palazzi, the look suited free-standing mansions like those that once faced Riverside Drive, as well as row houses from Murray Hill to the Upper Westside. With gaslights in the walls of every room, plus two indoor toilets, these brownstones defined the standards of modern convenience.
BEST SEEN: Scattered throughout Manhattan and Brooklyn; these are probably the most plentiful brownstones in New York.

ANGLO-ITALIANATE
ERA: 1850 to 1880
Distinguishing traits: Opulent interior decorations including carved ceilings, carved mantels, and parquet floors appealed to the new merchant class. By applying Italianate style carvings to the exterior brownstone, but repeating it across many buildings in the English fashion, this hybrid was born.
HISTORY: With two rooms on each floor, separated by doors that slide out of view, these highly desirable brownstones provided

flexibility for entertaining, and confinement when retaining fireplace heat in winter. These were the first houses to feature closets, with pegs on three sides to hang clothing, as well as dumbwaiters, gas cooking, and hot-air furnaces.

BEST SEEN ON: 16th Street between Second and Third avenues, 70th Street off Central Park West, and West 9th, 10th, and 12th Streets off lower Fifth Avenue (notably Renwick Terrace, 20-38 West 10th Street).

NEO-GREC

ERA: 1870 to 1900

Distinguishing traits: Foregoing the stoop, a new formality is introduced. Guests enter on street level into first floor reception rooms, often featuring grand staircases. Exteriors use a variety of materials, all culminating in the bold cornices atop each building. When Thomas Edison successfully generated electricity to Manhattan subscribers in 1882, a new modern architecture was born, which soon included elevators, and previously un-imaginable kitchen amenities.

HISTORY: Unlike the protruding ornamentation seen on many west-side brownstones, a new understated look of incising into the stone and glass, known as the "Eastlake motif" and "Neo-Grec fluting," is introduced on these elegant townhouses. Built deeply on their lots, with little outdoor space, these dense buildings are costly to maintain, but highly desirable for foundations, private clubs, medical offices, embassies, and consulates.

BEST SEEN IN: East 70s between Fifth and Park avenues; often the most costly townhouses on the market, due to their size, location, and rarity.

QUEEN ANNE

ERA: 1870 to 1900

Distinguishing traits: Breaking the symmetry of earlier construction, rows of Queen Anne style houses are constructed of the same materials, but each exterior varies in design. The result is a visually exciting challenge to the norm.

HISTORY: As America contemplated its Centennial in 1876, an interest in its early architecture re-emerged. Breaking the sleekness of Neo-Grec designs, Queen Anne houses are smaller than most Federal houses, but are notable for the intricate "gingerbread" ornamentation inside and out. While carved garlands may be back on the facade, many Queen Anne houses forego the cornices on top in exchange for pointed or stepped rooflines, each of them different from their neighbors. Ceilings are low, stairs are narrow, but Queen Annes are the jewels of townhouse design.

BEST SEEN IN: East 80s, near York Avenue.

Eventually, New Yorkers tired of the monumental streetscapes and showy ornamentation of row houses. They tired of the stairs, the sooty fireplaces, and the limited storage space.

Blame it on The Dakota: When America's first luxury apartment house opened in 1884, the real estate market went spinning in an exciting new direction. Filled with as much ornamentation as a block of Queen Anne townhouses, The Dakota offered spacious homes without stairs, luxurious bathrooms, and something that townhouse owners never considered: views. While townhouses were constructed sporadically over the ensuing years, the arrival of luxury apartments slowed new townhouse construction. Rows of them were razed to make room for new high-rise construction, as more people squeezed into New York's five boroughs. Freestanding mansions toppled too, as developers met the demand for luxury apartment construction.

Today, the finite number of townhouses remaining in New York comprises some of its most valuable real estate. With more than half of Manhattan's townhouses protected by landmark status, they're also a romantic reminder of the city's history.

Bibliography

Anbinder, Tyler, Five Points, The Free Press, New York, 2001.

Baker, Paul R., Stanny: The Gilded Life of Stanford White, The Free Press, a division of MacMillan Inc., New York, 1989.

Batterberry, Michael and Ariane, On The Town In New York, Scribner, New York, 1973.

Beard, Rick, and Berlowitz, Leslie Cohen, editors, Greenwich Village: Culture and Counterculture, published for the Museum of the City of New York by Rutgers University Press, New Brunswick, New Jersey, 1993.

Birmingham, Stephen, Life At The Dakota, Random House, NY 1979.

Bookbinder, Bernie, City of the World: New York and its People, Harry N. Abrams, Inc. New York, 1989.

Brown, Henry Collins, Fifth Avenue Old and New, official publication of the Fifth Avenue Association, Wynkoop Hallenbeck Crawford Co., New York, 1924.

Casill, Peter, New York Memories of Yesteryear, Exposition Press, New York, 1964.

Caro, Robert A., The Power Broker, Knopf, New York, 1989.

Daley, Robert, The World Beneath the City, J.B. L:ippincott Company, Philadelphia and New York, 1959.

Delaney, Edmund T., New York's Turtle Bay – Old and New, Barre Publishers, Barre, Massachusetts, 1965.

Dunlop, M. H., Gilded City, HarperCollins Publishers, Inc. New York, 2000.

Ellis, Edward Robb, The Epic of New York City, Coward Mc-

Cann Inc., New York, 1966.

Federal Writers Project, New York City Guide, Random House, New York, 1939.

Federal Writers Project, New York Panorama, Random House, New York, 1938.

Foreman, John, and Pierce Stimson, Robbe. The Vanderbilts and the Gilded Age, New York: St. Martins Press, 1991.

Garmey, Stephen, Gramercy Park: An Illustrated History of a New York Neighborhood, Balsam Press Inc., Rutledge Books, New York, 1984.

Gayle, Margot, and Gillon, Edmund V., Cast-Iron Architecture in New York, Dover Publications, Inc., New York, 1974.

Gaylord, R. Bruce Cranor, The Picture Book of Greenwich Village, Carol Publishing Group, New York 1991.

George-Warren, Holly, editor: The Rolling Stone Book of the Beats, Rolling Stone Press, New York, 1999.

Goldstone, Harmon H., History Preserved: A Guide to New York City Landmarks, Simon and Schuster, New York, 1974.

Greenberg, Cheryl Lynn, "Or Does It Explode?" Black Harlem In The Great Depression, Oxford University Press, New York, 1997.

Gurock, Jeffrey S., When Harlem Was Jewish, Columbia University Press, New York 1979.

Hanley, Rev. Denis J., A Pictorial History of Early Chinatown, ARTS Inc., New York, 1980.

Hindus, Milton, The Old East Side, an Anthology, The

Jewish Publication Society of America, Philadelphia, PA, 1969.

Homberger, Eric, The Historical Atlas of New York City, Henry Holt and Company, New York, 1994.

Jackson, Kenneth T., et.al. The Encyclopedia of New York City, New York Historical Society/Yale University Press, New Haven, 1995.

Jackson, Kenneth T., and Dunbar, David S., Empire City: New York Through the Centuries, Columbia University Press, New York, 2002.

Jacob Riis. (n.d.). Retrieved October 28, 2009, from http://en.wikipedia.org/wiki/Jacob_Riis

Janvier, Thomas A., In Old New York, Harper & Brothers, New York, 1894. Reprinted by St. Martin's Press, New York, April 2000.

King, Robert B. The Vanderbilt Homes, New York: Rizzoli International Publications, 1989.

Kahn, Steve, SoHo New York, Rizzoli International Publications Inc., New York, 1999.

Lanier, Henry Wysham, Greenwich Village, Today and Yesterday, Harper and Brothers, New York, 1949.

Lockwood, Charles, Bricks and Brownstone, Abbeville Press, New York, 1972.

Lockwood, Charles, Manhattan Moves Uptown, Houghton Mifflin Company, Boston, Massachusetts, 1976.

Lowe, David, Stanford White's New York, Doubleday, NY 1992

Lyman, Susan Elizabeth, The Story of New York, Crown Publishers, New York, 1964.

Miller, Terry, Greenwich Village And How It Got That Way, Crown Publishers Inc. New York, 1990.

Mitgang, Herbert, Once Upon A Time In New York, The Free Press, a division of Simon & Schuster, New York, 2000.

Moorhouse, Geoffrey, Imperial City: New York, Henry Holt and Company, New York 1988.

Patterson, Jerry E., Fifth Avenue: The Best Address, Rizzoli International Publications, Inc., New York, 1998.

Perlman, Bennard B., Painters of the Ashcan School, Dover Publications Inc., New York 1979.

Plumb, Stephen, The Streets Where They Lived, MarLor Press, St. Paul, MN, 1989.
Roskolenko, Harry, The Time

That Was Then, The Dial Press, New York, 1971.

Rosenzweig, Roy and Blackmar, Elizabeth, The Park and the People, Cornell University Press, Ithaca, New York, 1992.

Ruttenbaum, Steven, Mansions in the Clouds: the Skyscraper Palazzi of Emery Roth, Balsam Press, New York 1986.

Salwen, Peter, Upper West Side Story, Abbeville Press, NY 1989.

Shaw, Arnold, The Street That Never Slept, Coward, McCann & Geoghan, Inc. New York, 1971.

Silverberg, Robert, Light For The World, D. Van Nostrand Company Inc., New York, 1967.

Tauranac, John, Essential New York, Holt Rineholt & Winston,

NY 1980.

Trager, James, Park Avenue: Street of Dreams, Atheneum, NY 1990.

Trager, James, West of Fifth: The Rise and Fall and Rise of Manhattan's West Side, Atheneum, NY 1987.

Willensky, Eliot and White, Norval, American Institute of Architects Guide to New York City, third edition, Harcourt Brace Jovanovich, New York, 1988.

Wolfe, Gerard, New York: A Guide To The Metropolis, NY University Press, NY, 1978.

Wurman, Richard Saul, Access: New York City, HarperCollins, New York, 1997

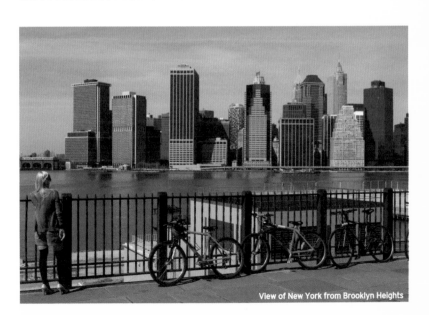

View of New York from Brooklyn Heights

INDEX

ABOUT MUSEYON

Named after the Museion, the ancient Egyptian institute dedicated to the muses, Museyon
Guides is an independent publisher that explores the world through the lens of cultural
obsessions. Intended for frequent fliers and armchair travelers alike, our books are expert-
curated and carefully researched, offering rich visuals, practical tips, and quality information.
Pick one up and follow your interests ... wherever they might go.

Chronicles of Old New York	9780982232064
Chronicles of Old Boston	9780984633401
Chronicles of Old Las Vegas	9780984633418
Chronicles of Old Paris	9780984633425
Chronicles of Old London	9780984633432
Chronicles of Old Rome	9780984633449

Publisher: Akira Chiba
Editor-in-Chief: Heather Corcoran

Art Director: Ray Yuen
Cover Design: José Antonio Contreras

For more information visit **www.museyon.com**

ACKNOWLEDGEMENTS

Museyon Guides would like to thank the following individuals and organizations for their guidance and assistance in creating *Chronicles of Old New York.*

Lower East Side Tenement Museum

Museum of the City of New York

National Park Service, Frederick Law Olmsted National Historic Site

New-York Historical Society

New York Public Library

New York University Archives

Prints & Photographs Division, Library of Congress

Public Theater

Smithsonian Institution, National Portrait Gallery

Susan S. Szenasy, *Metropolis* Magazine

Brey Brownlie, *New York Living* Magazine

Karolina Pierz, *New York Living* Magazine

Ann Simkins, *New York Living* Magazine

Janice Battiste, *New York Living* Magazine

Taka Hayashi, Pepperland

PHOTO CREDITS

Pages 4-5: View of New York from Brooklyn Heights, 1849

Picture Collection, The New York Public Library, Astor, Lenox and Tilden Foundations

Page 6: Plan de New-York et des environs / levé par Montresor, igénieur en 1775, 1777

The Lionel Pincus and Princess Firyal Map Division, The New York Public Library, Astor, Lenox and Tilden Foundations

Page 10: L.W. Schmidt, Bird's eye view of the city of New York

Popular Graphic Arts Collection, Prints & Photographs Division, Library of Congress, LC-DIG-pga-04130

Page 12: Chappel, Alonzo. Washington's farewell to his officers, 1783

Picture Collection, The New York Public Library, Astor, Lenox and Tilden Foundations

Page 15: Hollyer, Samuel. George Washington's house, Cherry Street, N.Y.C., 1788

Picture Collection, The New York Public Library, Astor, Lenox and Tilden Foundations

Page16: Krimmel, John Lewis. Barroom Dancing, ca. 1820

Drawings (documentary) Collection, Prints & Photographs Division, Library of Congress, LC-DIG-ppmsca-22808

Page 18: Hill, John William. City Hall and Park Row, 1830

I.N. Phelps Stokes Collection, Miriam and Ira D. Wallach Division of Art, Prints and Photographs, The New York Public Library, Astor, Lenox and Tilden Foundations

Fay, Augustus. Croton Water Reservoir, New York City, 1850.

I.N. Phelps Stokes Collection, Miriam and Ira D. Wallach Division of Art, Prints and Photographs, The New York Public Library, Astor, Lenox and Tilden Foundations

Page 21: Vanderlyn, John. Aaron Burr, 1802

Page 24: Portraits of Kiralfy family and lead dancers

with scenes from productions, ca.1873

Posters: Performing Arts Collection, Prints & Photographs Division, Library of Congress, POS-TH-KIR, no. 26

Page 26: Bookhout, Edward. Burr's residence near New York, 1880

Emmet Collection, Miriam and Ira D. Wallach Division of Art, Prints and Photographs, The New York Public Library, Astor, Lenox and Tilden Foundations

Page 30: The original wooden arch, 1889

New York University Archives, Photographic Collection

Page 33: Nueva York—las fiestas del centenario de Washington: paso de la procesón civica por la Quinta Avenida, el 3 del corriente, 1889

Picture Collection, The New York Public Library, Astor, Lenox and Tilden Foundations

Page 35: Rogers, William Allen. A stage in the thirties, 1892

Cabinet of American Illustration, Prints & Photographs Division, Library of Congress, LC-USZ62-87654

Page 37: Smedley, W.T. Easter Sunday of Fifth Avenue, 1890

Cabinet of American Illustration, Prints & Photographs Division, Library of Congress, LC-USZ62-118834

Hyde, J.N. New York City—An Afternoon lounge at Goupil's Art Gallery, Fifth Avenue, 1872

Miscellaneous Items in High Demand Collection, Prints & Photographs Division, Library of Congress, LC-USZ62-120368

Ladies' drawing-room in the Fifth Avenue Hotel, 1859

Miscellaneous Items in High Demand Collection, Prints & Photographs Division, Library of Congress, LC-USZ62-73675

Page 38: Mrs Astor Greeting Guests at her Ball, 1903

© Bettmann / CORBIS

Page 42: Astor House

Popular Graphic Arts Collection, Prints & Photographs Division, Library of Congress, LC-USZ62-62198

Page 46: Currier, Nathaniel. Great riot at the Astor Place Opera House, New York: on Thursday evening May 10th 1849, 1849

Popular Graphic Arts Collection, Prints & Photographs Division, Library of Congress, LC-USZC2-2532

Page 48: Smillie, James. Junction of Broadway and the Bowery, 1831

I.N. Phelps Stokes Collection, Miriam and Ira D. Wallach Division of Art, Prints and Photographs, The New York Public Library, Astor, Lenox and Tilden Foundations

Page 49: Grace Church, between 1901 and 1906

Detroit Publishing Company Photograph Collection, Prints & Photographs Division, Library of Congress, LC-D4-9033

Page 51: Jukes, Francis. New York from Hobuck Ferry House New Jersey, 1800

Popular Graphic Arts Collection, Prints & Photographs Division, Library of Congress, LC-USZ62-1238

Heine, J. Kummer & Döpler. New York, 1851

Popular Graphic Arts Collection, Prints & Photographs Division, Library of Congress, LC-DIG-ppmsca-08310

Page 52: Lawrence, Richard Hoe. Bandit's Roost, 59 1/2 Mulberry St., ca. 1890

Museum of the City of New York, Jacob A. Riis Collection, Gift of Roger William Riis, 1990

Page 55: W. Endicott & Co. The old brewery at the Five Points, N.Y., 1852

Eno Collection, Miriam and Ira D. Wallach Division of Art, Prints and Photographs, The New York Public Library, Astor, Lenox and Tilden Foundations

Page 56: Five Points 1827, Intersection of Cross, Anthony and Orange Streets, from Valentine's Manual, 1855, page 112; negative no. 44668

Collection of The New-York Historical Society

Page 57: Policeman leading upper class people through the Five Points neighborhood, 1885

Miscellaneous Items in High Demand Collection, Prints & Photographs Division, Library of Congress, LC-USZ62-1226600

Page 58: Johnston, Frances Benjamin. Jacob Riis, ca. 1900

Johnston (Frances Benjamin) Collection, Prints & Photographs Division, Library of Congress, LC-USZ62-47078

Page 59: Riis, Jacob. Street Arabs in sleeping quarters, ca. 1888

Miscellaneous Items in High Demand Collection, Prints & Photographs Division, Library of Congress, LC-USZ62-39057

Page 62: Snyder, W. P. Operating-room, Edison Station, New York, 1896

Picture Collection, The New York Public Library, Astor, Lenox and Tilden Foundations

Page 65: Thomas Edison, full-length portrait, seated, facing front, with phonograph, ca. 1878

Miscellaneous Items in High Demand Collection, Prints & Photographs Division, Library of Congress, LC-USZ62-98128

Page 66: Home of Mrs. J.P. Morgan, 231 Madison Avenue, New York City, 1913

Bain Collection, Prints & Photographs Division, Library of Congress, LC-USZ62-98994

Page 68: Kilburn, Lawrence. James Beekman, 1761

Collection of The New-York Historical Society

Page 70: Beekman House, residence of Sir William Howe, 1776. Fiftieth Street near First Avenue, 1897

Picture Collection, The New York Public Library, Astor, Lenox and Tilden Foundations

Page 72: Jaques, Ted. 3rd Ave. looking South from 55th St., 1948

Museum of the City of New York, Gift of the artist

Page 74: Hawley, Hughson. Granite pavement of Fifth Avenue at Thirty-ninth Street, New York, 1889.

Picture Collection, The New York Public Library, Astor, Lenox and Tilden Foundations

Page 77: Fifth Avenue, 1906

Detroit Publishing Company Collection, Prints & Photographs Collection, Library of Congress, LC-D$-15514 R

Page 78: Delmonico's, New York, ca. 1903

Detroit Publishing Company Collection, Prints & Photographs Division, Library of Congress, LC-D4-16669

Page 79: Dinner for Mark Twain, 1905

Museum of the City of New York, Byron Collection, Gift of Percy Byron, 1942

Page 82: View of the Beam Tunnel from 59th to 76th Street, Fourth Avenue, New York City. From Leslie's Monthly Magazine, 1876

Picture Collection, The New York Public Library, Astor, Lenox and Tilden Foundations

Page 84: Jackson, William Henry. Grand Central Station [i.e. Depot], 1921

Detroit Publishing Company Collection, Prints & Photographs Division, Library of Congress, LC-D4-13387

Page 85: Brady, Matthew. Cornelius Vanderbilt, head-and-shoulders portrait, slightly to left, with side whiskers, ca. 1844-1860

Daguerreotypes Collection, Prints & Photographs Division, Library of Congress, LC-USZC4-4160

Page 86: The sunken track of the N.Y. and Harlem Railroad, 4th Avenue, above 126 Street, New York City, 1876

Picture Collection, The New York Public Library, Astor, Lenox and Tilden Foundations

Page 88: Vanderbilt Ball, Mrs. Cornelius Vanderbilt as electric light, March 26, 1883, photo by Mora; Costume Ball Photograph Collection, PR-223, Series V, Folder 34; negative no. 39500

Collection of the New-York Historical Society

Page 91: Mayor Gaynor, Col. Roosevelt and Cornelius Vanderbilt on 5th Ave, 1910.

Miscellaneous Items in High Demand Collection, Prints & Photographs Division, Library of Congress, LC-USZ62-60851

Page 92: Houses and mansions - Vanderbilt Mansion. Wedding day of Gladys Vanderbilt and Count Laszlo Szechenyi, Jan. 28, 1908, 1908

Bain Collection, Prints & Photographs Division, Library of Congress, LC-USZ62-69597

Page 94: Wyand, D.E. The Squatters of New York-scene near Central Park, 1869

Miscellaneous Items in High Demand Collection, Prints & Photographs Division, Library of Congress, LC-USZ62-106378

Page 97: Grand Drive, Central Park N.Y., 1869, Published by Currier & Ives

Museum of the City of New York, The Harry T. Peters Collection

Page 98: Olmsted Family Photographs, Olmsted Job #1 Frederick Law Olmsted Sr. cap & cape c. 1860

Courtesy of the Nation Park Service, Frederick Law Olmsted National Historic Site

Page 100: New York City-serenade given to ex-governor Tilden at his Gramercy Park residence on October 27th 1877

Picture Collection, The New York Public Library, Astor, Lenox and Tilden Foundations

Page 103: Abbott, Berenice. Gramercy Park North #60

Milstein Division of United States History, Local History & Genealogy, The New York Public Library, Astor, Lenox and Tilden Foundations

Page 105: See Page 167: Cab stand at Madison Square, 1900

Detroit Publishing Company Collection, Prints & Photographs Division, Library of Congress, LC-D401-13619

Flatiron Building, New York, N.Y., 1902

Detroit Publishing Company Collection, Prints & Photographs Division, Library of Congress, LC-D401-14278

Clam seller in Mulberry Bend, N.Y., 1900

Detroit Publishing Company Collection, Prints & Photographs Division, Library of Congress, LC-D401-13642

Newsboys and newsgirl. (Mary Malchade) (9 years old.) Getting afternoon papers, Park Row, 1910

National Child Labor Committee Collection, Prints & Photographs Division, Library of Congress, LC-USZ62-120557

On the streets in a New York blizzard, 1899

Detroit Publishing Company Collection, Prints & Photographs Division, Library of Congress, LC-D4-13621

Hine, Lewis Wickes. Tending Stand, Canal St. Location, 1910

National Child Labor Committee Collection, Prints & Photographs Division, Library of Congress, LC-USZ6-1242

Hine, Lewis Wickes. A load of kimonos just finished. Girl very reticent. Thompson St., N.Y., 1912

National Child Labor Committee Collection, Prints & Photographs Division, Library of Congress, LC-DIG-nclc-05490

Miss Twombly, whip of Ladies Coach Run, and two other ladies beside coach on street, New York

Bain Collection, Prints & Photographs Division, Library of Congress, LC-DIG-ggbain-03305

Page 106: Madison Square Garden, New York, N.Y.

Detroit Publishing Company Photograph Collection, Prints & Photographs Division, Library of Congress, LC-D4-12672

Page 109: Käsebier, Gertrude. Evelyn Nesbit about 1900 at a time when she was brought to the studio by Stanford White, 1900

Miscellaneous Items in High Demand Collection, Prints & Photographs Division, Library of Congress, LC-DIG-ppmsca-12056

Page 110: Mrs. Thos. Hastings's coach leaves Colony Club. 5/10/11. Mrs. A. Iselin, whip, Mrs. Hastings beside her, Mrs. W.G. Loew behind

Bain Collection, Prints & Photographs Division, Library of Congress, LC-B2-2230-17

Penn Station, New York City, 1920

Miscellaneous Items in High Demand, Prints & Photographs Division, Library of Congress, LC-USZ62-74598

Zane, Steven. Villard Houses, 451-457 Madison Avenue & 24 East Fifty-first Street, New York, New York County, NY

Historic American Buildings Survey/Historic American Engineering Record/Historic American Landscapes Survey Collection, Prints & Photographs Division, Library of Congress, HABS NY, 31-NEYO, 120-

Page 112: Draper, John William. Dorothy Draper, 1840

New York University Archives, Photographic Collection

Page 116: De Meyer, Adolf, Baron. Three-quarter length portrait of Gertrude Vanderbilt Whitney (Mrs. Harry Payne Whitney) wearing a jeweled gown and tiara and holding a peacock feather fan, 1916

Johnston (Francis Benjamin Collection) / PH Filing Series Photographs Collection, Prints & Photographs Division, Library of Congress, LC-USZC2-6127

Page 118: Manhattan: Central Park West, west side btw. 72nd Street and 73rd Street

Milstein Division of United States History, Local History & Genealogy, The New York Public Library, Astor, Lenox and Tilden Foundations

Page 125: Collins, Marjory. New York, New York. Central Park common on Sunday.

Farm Security Administration/Office of War Information Black-and-White Negatives, Prints & Photographs Division, Library of Congress, LC-USW3-007791-E

258

Page 128:Sunday morning at Orchard and Rivington, New York City, 1915

Bain Collection, Prints & Photographs Division, Library of Congress, LC-USZ62-72444

Page 130:Hine, Lewis Wickes. 1 P.M. Family of Onofrio Cottone, 7 Extra Pl., N.Y., finishing garments in a terribly run down tenement. The father works on the street. The three oldest children help the mother on garments. Joseph, 14, Andrew, 10, Rosie, 7, and all together they make about $2 a week when work is plenty. There are two babies. 1913

National Child Labor Committee Collection, Prints & Photographs Division, Library of Congress, LC-DIG-nclc-04305

Niwa, Keiko. Lower East Side Tenement Museum

Courtesy Lower East Side Tenement Museum

Page 132: New York City Deputy Police Commissioner John A. Leach, right, watching agents pour liquor into sewer following a raid during the height of prohibition, 1921

Miscellaneous Items in High Demand Collection, Prints & Photographs Division, Library of Congress, LC-USZ62-123257

Page 135: Van Vechten, Carl. Portrait of Bill Robinson, 1933

Van Vechten Collection, Prints & Photographs Division, Library of Congress, LC-DIG-ppmsca-18631

Page 138: Crowd outside the Savoy in Harlem

© Bettmann/CORBIS

Page 144: Abbott, Berenice. Triborough Bridge, East 125th Street approach, Manhattan, 1937

Photography Collection, Miriam and Ira D. Wallach Division of Art, Prints and Photographs, The New York Public Library, Astor, Lenox and Tilden Foundations

Page 147: Spieglitz, C.M. Sponsor of Battery Bridge/World Telegram & Sun

Miscellaneous Items in High Demand Collection, Prints & Photographs Division, Library of Congress, LC-USZ62-136079

Page 152: Ginsberg, Allen. William S. Burroughs, Lucien Carr and Allen Ginsberg, 1953

© Allen Ginsberg/CORBIS

Page 155: Vachon, John. New York, New York. Times Square on a rainy day, 1943

Farm Security Administration/Office of War Information Black-and-White Negatives, Prints & Photographs Division, Library of Congress, LC-USW3-020251-E

Page 158: Broadway, North from Spring Street, 1898

Museum of the City of New York, Byron Collection, Gift of Percy Byron, 1942

Page 161: Rau, William H. Busy Broadway, north from Prince Street, New York City, 1904

Stereograph Cards Collection, Prints & Photographs Division, Library of Congress, LC-USZ62-94237

Page 162: The first cast-iron house erected at New York, from The Illustrated London News, 1851

Pictures Collection, The New York Public Library, Astor, Lenox and Tilden Foundations

Page 164: Abbott, Berenice. West Washington Market, Washington Street and Loew Avenue, Manhattan, 1936

Photography Collection, Miriam and Ira D. Wallach Division of Art, Prints and Photographs, The New York Public Library, Astor, Lenox and Tilden Foundations

Washington Market, 1895

Museum of the City of New York, Byron Collection

Page 167:Grand Central Station and Hotel Manhattan, 1900-1906

Detroit Publishing Company Collection, Prints & Photographs Division, Library of Congress, LC-D4-11720

The Bowery, 1900

Detroit Publishing Company Collection, Prints & Photographs Division, Library of Congress, LC-D4-12529

Shoppers on Sixth Avenue, 1903

Detroit Publishing Company Collection, Prints & Photographs Division, Library of Congress, LC-D4-9145

Page 168: Chelsea Hotel, 1936

Photograph by Berenice Abbott

Museum of the City of New York, Gift of Federal Works Agency, Work Projects Administration, Federal Art Project, 1943

Page 170: Clement C. Moore by Matthew Brady Studio

National Portrait Gallery, Smithsonian Institution, Frederick Hill Meserve Collection, Meserve.1127:40

Page 172: Gottscho, Samuel H. New York City views. Rockefeller Center and RCA Building from 515 Madison Ave., 1933

Gottscho-Schleisner Collection, Prints & Photographs Division, Library of Congress, LC-G612-T01-21012-Ax

Page 175: Firemen searching for bodies, 1911

Bain Collection, Prints & Photographs Division, Library of Congress, LC-USZ62-83864

Page 176: Harris & Ewing. U.S. Ambassador to Great Britain. Washington, D.C., Dec. 9, 1939

Harris & Ewing Collection, Prints & Photographs Division, Library of Congress, LC-H22-D-7951

Page 177: John D. Rockefeller, full-length portrait, walking on street with John D. Rockefeller, Jr., 1915

Miscellaneous Items in High Demand Collection, Prints & Photographs Division, Library of Congress, LC-USZ62-48511

Page 180: City Hall, New York

Detroit Publishing Company Photograph Collection, Prints & Photographs Division, Library of Congress, LC-D4-17237

Page 188: Fraunce's Tavern, Broad and Pearl Streets, New York, 1900-1906

Detroit Publishing Company Collection, Prints & Photographs Division, Library of Congress, LC-D4-16368

Page 189: Types of Life on the Promenade, Brooklyn Bridge, N.Y., 1904

Stereograph Cards, Prints & Photographs Division, Library of Congress, LC-USZ62-56629

Jefferson Market Court House, New York, 1905

Detroit Publishing Company Collection, Prints & Photographs Division, LC-D401-18604

Longacre Square, 1904

Miscellaneous Items in High Demand Collection,

Prints & Photographs Division, Library of Congress, LC-USZ62-77320

Page 190: Mulberry Street, New York City, 1900

Detroit Publishing Company Collection, Prints & Photographs Division, Library of Congress, LC-D401-12683

Page 198: Abbott, Berenice. Milk wagon and old houses, Grove Street, No. 4-10, Manhattan, 1936

Photography Collection, Miriam and Ira D. Wallach Division of Art, Prints and Photographs, The New York Public Library, Astor, Lenox and Tilden Foundations

Page 206: Hine, Lewis Wickers. The breaking point. A heavy load for an old woman. Lafayette St., below Astor Pl., N.Y., 1912

National Child Labor Committee Collection, Prints & Photographs Division, Library of Congress, LC-DIG-nclc-04165

Page 211: Courtesy of the Public Theater

Dick, Archibald L. after, James H. Darkin. La Grange Terrace, La Fayette Place, City of New York. [1831-1834]

I.N. Phelps Stokes Collection, Miriam and Ira D. Wallach Division of Art, Prints and Photographs, The New York Public Library, Astor, Lenox and Tilden Foundations

Page 213: Gottscho, Samuel, H. New York city views. Night view of plaza buildings, over park lake, night, 1933

Gottscho-Schleisner Collection, Prints & Photographs Division, Library of Congress, LC-G612-T01-19557

Vachon, John. New York, New York. Camel cigarette advertisement at Times Square, 1943

Farm Security Administration/Office of War Information Black-and-White Negatives, Prints & Photographs Division, Library of Congress, LC-USW3-018258-D

Mott Street, New York, N.Y., 1905

Detroit Publishing Company Collection, Prints & Photographs Division, Library of Congress, LC-D4-18616

Page 214: Abbott, Berenice. Gramercy Park, nos. 3-5, Manhattan, 1935

Photography Collection, Miriam and Ira D. Wallach Division of Art, Prints and Photographs, The New York Public Library, Astor, Lenox and Tilden Foundations

Page 220: Gottscho, Samuel H. River House, 52nd St. and E. River, New York City. Cloud study, noon, looking south from 27th floor

Gottscho-Schleisner Collection, Prints & Photographs Division, Library of Congress, LC-G612-T01-17489

Page 228: Photo: Don Pollard

Courtesy of the New York Public Library

Page 232: The Dakota (Apartments), 1 West Seventy-second Street, Central Park West, New York, New York County, NY

Historic American Buildings Survey/Historic American Engineering Record/Historic American Landscapes Survey, Prints & Photographs Division, Library of Congress, HABS NY,31-NEYO, 74-

Page 236: Untitled [Harlem street scene], 1944

Museum of the City of New York, Gift of the Department of Local Government, Public Record Office of South Australia

James Roman

A third-generation New Yorker, James Roman has regaled listeners with his chronicles of old New York as a real estate broker and sales manager for fifteen years in Manhattan, and as a lecturer at the Real Estate Board of New York and New York University. He served as Editorial Contributor to *New York Living* magazine for six years, and contributes regularly to publications that document emerging technology. Readers can find him on re-runs of the HBO television series *Six Feet Under*, a break he attributes more to luck than to acumen.